There is also an underplot to the play. Rogero and Claridiana, between whom an hereditary feud exists, celebrate their marriage on the same day. As they return from the church an altercation arises between the bridegrooms, but by the intervention of friends they are at length induced to declare that they will lay aside their hatred. These professions are marked with little sincerity, for the new-made friends are intent upon cornuting one another. The wives, who are excellent friends, take counsel together and devise a scheme by which the husbands, while taking their lawful pleasure, imagine that they are tasting the sweets of adultery. Claridiana, announcing that he has gone to his farm in the country, repairs by appointment to the house of Rogero, where, under the impression that he is enjoying Rogero's wife Thais, he lies with his own wife Abigail; and Rogero, under Claridiana's roof lies with Thais in the belief that he is clipping Abigail. While these night-sports are in progress, Mendoza, nephew of the Duke Amago, holds a clandestine interview with the widowed Lady Lentulus. As he is mounting to her chamber, the rope-ladder breaks. Injured by the fall, he drags himself some distance from the house to a spot where he is discovered by the watch. It is supposed that he has met with foul play; a search is instituted; Rogero is discovered by the watch in the house of Claridiana, and Claridiana in the house of Rogero. Charged before the Duke Amago with the murder of Mendoza they declare themselves guilty—preferring to be hanged as murderers rather than to be derided as cuckolds. Mendoza, recovering from the effects of his fall, asserts (in order to save the honour of the Lady Lentulus) that he met his injuries in trying to steal some jewels from her house. The Duke, who is in a maze of wonder at the strange statements and confessions, condemns the three prisoners to be executed, hoping by this means to extort from them the truth. On the day fixed for the execution Thais and Abigail make an explanation to the Duke; and their husbands—finding that they have not been cuckolded—are glad to spare the hangman his labour. How Mendoza fares is not stated.

DRAMATIS PERSONÆ
Amago, Duke of Venice
Duke of Medina
Roberto, Count of Cyprus
Count Massino
Guido, Count of Arsena
Gniaca, Count of Gazia
Mendoza Foscari, nephew to Amago
Signior Mizaldus
Claridiana
Rogero
Don Sago, a Spanish Colonel
Cardinal
Isabella, the Insatiate Countess
Lady Lentulus, a widow
Abigail, wife to Claridiana
Thais, wife to Rogero
Anna, waiting-woman to Isabella
Senators, captain, lieutenant, soldiers, messenger, executioner, &c.

SCENE:—Venice and Pavia

ACT I

SCENE I

Venice.—Room in Isabella's house.

ISABELLA, Countess of Suevia, discovered sitting at a table covered with black, on which stands two black tapers lighted, she in mourning.

[Enter **ROBERTO**, Count of Cyprus, **GUIDO**, Count of Arsena, and **SIGNIOR MIZALDUS**.

MIZALDUS
What should we do in this countess's dark hole?
She's sullenly retirèd as the turtle.
Every day has been
A black day with her since her husband died;
And what should we unruly members make here?

GUIDO
As melancholy night masks up heaven's face,
So doth the evening star present herself
Unto the careful shepherd's gladsome eyes,
By which unto the fold he leads his flock.

MIZALDUS
Zounds! what a sheepish beginning is here? 'Tis said true love is simple; and it may well hold; and thou art a simple lover.

ROBERTO
See how yond star, like beauty in a cloud,
Illumines darkness, and beguiles the moon
Of all her glory in the firmament!

MIZALDUS
Well said, man i' the moon. Was ever such astronomers? Marry, I fear none of these will fall into the right ditch.

ROBERTO
Madam.

ISABELLA
Ha, Anna! what, are my doors unbarr'd?

The Insatiate Countess by John Marston

A Tragedie: Acted at White-Fryers

John Marston was born to John and Maria Marston née Guarsi, and baptised on October 7th, 1576 at Wardington, Oxfordshire.

Marston entered Brasenose College, Oxford in 1592 and earned his BA in 1594. By 1595, he was in London, living in the Middle Temple. His interests were in poetry and play writing, although his father's will of 1599 hopes that he would not further pursue such vanities.

His brief career in literature began with the fashionable genres of erotic epyllion and satire; erotic plays for boy actors to be performed before educated young men and members of the inns of court.

In 1598, he published 'The Metamorphosis of Pigmalion's Image and Certaine Satyres', a book of poetry. He also published 'The Scourge of Villanie', in 1598.

'Histriomastix' regarded as his first play was produced 1599. It's performance kicked off an episode in literary history known as the War of the Theatres; a literary feud between Marston, Jonson and Dekker that lasted until 1602.

However, the playwrights were later reconciled; Marston wrote a prefatory poem for Jonson's 'Sejanus' in 1605 and dedicated 'The Malcontent' to him.

Beyond this episode Marston's career continued to gather both strength, assets and followers. In 1603, he became a shareholder in the Children of Blackfriars company. He wrote and produced two plays with the company. The first was 'The Malcontent' in 1603, his most famous play. His second was 'The Dutch Courtesan', a satire on lust and hypocrisy, in 1604-5.

In 1605, he worked with George Chapman and Ben Jonson on 'Eastward Ho', a satire of popular taste and the vain imaginings of wealth to be found in the colony of Virginia.

Marston took the theatre world by surprise when he gave up writing plays in 1609 at the age of thirty-three. He sold his shares in the company of Blackfriars. His departure from the literary scene may have been because of further offence he gave to the king. The king suspended performances at Blackfriars and had Marston imprisoned.

On 24th September 1609 he was made a deacon and them a priest on 24th December 1609. In October 1616, Marston was assigned the living of Christchurch, Hampshire.

He died (accounts vary) on either the 24th or 25th June 1634 in London and was buried in the Middle Temple Church.

Index of Contents

STORY OF THE PLAY

Isabella, Countess of Suevia, being left a widow, proceeds with indecent haste to take a second husband, Roberto, Count of Cyprus. At a masqued dance given by the bridegroom's friends on the day of the wedding, Isabella falls in love with one of the masquers, whom she discovers to be the Count of Massino. She sends him a letter in which she proffers her love and summons him to her presence. With her paramour she flies to Pavia, where she meets Massino's friend Gniaca, Count of Gaza or Gazia. The Insatiate Countess immediately falls in love with Gniaca, who—though at first unwilling to wrong his friend—quickly yields to her blandishments. Returning from a hunting expedition Massino is denied admittance by Isabella. He gives vent to his indignation by penning bitter satirical verses, in which he proclaims to the world her inordinate lust. Enraged at this exposure, Isabella incites Gniaca to slay Massino. An encounter ensues between Gniaca and Massino, but after a few passes the combatants put up their weapons, hold a friendly colloquy, and part in peace. Isabella is furious and resolves to destroy both Gniaca and Massino. She employs the services of a Spanish colonel, Don Sago, who at first sight of her has been violently inflamed with passion. The colonel shoots Massino dead, is arrested, and, being brought before the Duke of Medina, makes full confession. Isabella is condemned to be beheaded. At the place of execution a strange friar requests that he may have private speech with her. The friar is Count Roberto, who has come to pronounce forgiveness, and bid a last farewell, to his erring wife.

MIZALDUS

I'll assure you the way into your ladyship is open.

ROBERTO

And God defend that any profane hand
Should offer sacrilege to such a saint!
Lovely Isabella, by this duteous kiss,
That draws part of my soul along with it,
Had I but thought my rude intrusion
Had waked the dove-like spleen harbour'd within you,
Life and my first-born should not satisfy
Such a transgression, worthy of a check;
But that immortals wink at my offence,
Makes me presume more boldly. I am come
To raise you from this so infernal sadness.

ISABELLA

My lord of Cyprus, do not mock my grief.
Tears are as due a tribute to the dead,
As fear to God, and duty unto kings,
Love to the just, or hate unto the wicked.

ROBERTO

Surcease;
Believe it is a wrong unto the gods.
They sail against the wind that wail the dead:
And since his heart hath wrestled with death's pangs,
From whose stern cave none tracts a backward path,
Leave to lament this necessary change,
And thank the gods, for they can give us good.

ISABELLA

I wail his loss! Sink him ten cubits deeper,
I may not fear his resurrection.
I will be sworn upon the Holy Writ
I mourn thus fervent 'cause he died no sooner:
He buried me alive,
And mewed me up like Cretan Dædalus,
And with wall-ey'd jealousy kept me from hope
Of any waxen wings to fly to pleasure;
But now his soul her Argus' eyes hath closed,
And I am free as air. You of my sex,
In the first flow of youth, use you the sweets
Due to your proper beauties, ere the ebb
And long wane of unwelcome change shall come.
Fair women, play; she's chaste whom none will have.
Here is a man of a most mild aspect,

Temperate, effeminate, and worthy love;
One that with burning ardor hath pursued me.
A donative he hath of every god:
Apollo gave him locks; Jove his high front;
The god of eloquence his flowing speech;
The feminine deities strew'd all their bounties
And beauty on his face; that eye was Juno's;
Those lips were hers that won the golden ball;
That virgin-blush, Diana's. Here they meet,
As in a sacred synod. My lords, I must intreat
A while your wish'd forbearance.

GUIDO and **MIZALDUS**
We obey you, lady.

[Exeunt **GUIDO** and **MIZALDUS**.

ISABELLA
My lord, with you I have some conference.
I pray, my lord, do you woo every lady
In this phrase you do me?

ROBERTO
Fairest, till now
Love was an infant in my oratory.

ISABELLA
And kiss thus too?

[Kisses him.

ROBERTO
I never was so kiss'd; leave thus to please;
Flames into flames, seas thou pour'st into seas!

ISABELLA
Pray frown, my lord: let me see how many wives You'll have.
Heigh ho! you'll bury me, I see—

ROBERTO
In the swan's down, and tomb thee in mine arms!

ISABELLA
Then folks shall pray in vain to send me rest.
Away, you're such another meddling lord!

ROBERTO
By heaven! my love's as chaste as thou art fair,

And both exceed comparison. By this kiss,
That crowns me monarch of another world
Superior to the first, fair, thou shalt see
As unto heaven my love, so unto thee!

ISABELLA
Alas!
Poor creatures, when we are once o' the falling hand,
A man may easily come over us.
It is as hard for us to hide our love
As to shut sin from the Creator's eyes.
I'faith, my lord, I had a month's mind unto you,
As tedious as a full-riped maiden-head;
And, Count of Cyprus, think my love as pure
As the first opening of the blooms in May:
(You're virtuous, man; nay, let me not blush to say so:)
And see for your sake thus I leave to sorrow.
Begin this subtile conjuration with me,
And as this taper, due unto the dead,
I here extinguish, so my late-dead lord
I put out ever from my memory,
That his remembrance may not wrong our love,

[Puts out the taper.

As bold-faced women, when they wed another,
Banquet their husbands with their dead loves' heads.

ROBERTO
And as I sacrifice this to his ghost,
With this expire all corrupt thoughts of youth,
That fame-insatiate devil jealousy,
And all the sparks that may bring unto flame,
Hate betwixt man and wife, or breed defame.

[Puts out the other taper.

[Re-enter **MIZALDUS** and **GUIDO**.

MIZALDUS
Marry, amen. I say; madam, are you that were in for all day, now come to be in for all night? How now, Count Arsena?

GUIDO
Faith, signior, not unlike the condemn'd malefactor,
That hears his judgment openly pronounced;
But I ascribe to fate. Joy swell your love;
Cypress and willow grace my drooping crest.

ROBERTO
We do intend our hymeneal rites
With the next rising sun. Count Arsena,
Next to our bride, the welcom'st to our feast.

[Exeunt **ISABELLA** and **ROBERTO**.

GUIDO
Sancta Maria! what think'st thou of this change?
A player's passion I'll believe hereafter,
And in a tragic scene weep for old Priam,
When fell-revenging Pyrrhus with supposed
And artificial wounds mangles his breast,
And think it a more worthy act to me,
Than trust a female mourning o'er her love.
Naught that is done of woman shall me please,
Nature's step-children, rather her disease.

MIZALDUS
Learn of a well-composèd epigram
A woman's love, and thus 'twas sung unto us;
The tapers that stood on her husband's hearse,
Isabel advances to a second bed:
Is it not wondrous strange for to rehearse
She should so soon forget her husband, dead
One hour? for if the husband's life once fade,
Both love and husband in one grave are laid.
But we forget ourselves: I am for the marriage
Of Signior Claridiana and the fine Mistress Abigail.

GUIDO
I for his arch-foe's wedding, Signior Rogero, and the spruce Mistress Thais: but see, the solemn rites are
ended, and from their several temples they are come.

MIZALDUS
A quarrel, on my life!

[Enter at one door **SIGNIOR CLARIDIANA**, **ABIGAIL** his wife, and the **LADY LENTULUS**, with rosemary, as
from church; at the other door **SIGNIOR ROGERO**, **THAIS** his wife, and **MENDOZA FOSCARI**, nephew to
the **DUKE**, from the bridal; they see one another, and draw; **GUIDO** and **OTHERS** step between them.

CLARIDIANA
Good, my lord, detain me not; I will tilt at him.

MIZALDUS
Remember, sir, this is your wedding-day,
And that triumph belongs only to your wife.

ROGERO
If you be noble, let me cut off his head.

GUIDO
Remember, o' the other side, you have a maiden-head of your own to cut off.

ROGERO
I'll make my marriage-day like to the bloody bridal
Alcides by the fiery Centaurs had!

THAIS
Husband, dear husband!

ROGERO
Away with these catterwallers!
Come on, sir.

CLARIDIANA
Thou son of a Jew!

GUIDO
Alas, poor wench, thy husband's circumcised!

CLARIDIANA
Begot when thy father's face was toward th' east,
To show that thou would'st prove a caterpiller.
His Messias shall not save thee from me;
I'll send thee to him in collops!

GUIDO
O fry not in choler so, sir!

ROGERO
Mountebank, with thy pedantical action—
Rimatrix, Bugloss, Rhinoceros!

MENDOZA
Gentlemen, I conjure you
By the virtues of men!

ROGERO
Shall any broken quacksalver's bastard oppose him to me in my nuptials? No; but I'll show him better metal than e'er the gallemawfrey his father used. Thou scum of his melting-pots, that wert christen'd in a crusoile with Mercury's water to show thou wouldest prove a stinging aspis! for all thou spitt'st is aqua fortis, and thy breath is a compound of poison's stillatory: if I get within thee, hadst thou the scaly hide of a crocodile, as thou art partly of his nature, I would leave thee as bare as an anatomy at the second viewing.

CLARIDIANA

Thou Jew of the tribe of Gad that, I were sure, were there none here but thou and I, wouldst teach me the art of breathing; thou wouldst run like a dromedary!

ROGERO

Thou that art the tall'st man of Christendom when thou art alone; if thou dost maintain this to my face, I'll make thee skip like an ounce.

MENDOZA

Nay, good sir, be you still.

ROGERO

Let the quacksalver's son be still:
His father was still, and still, and still again!

CLARIDIANA

By the Almighty, I'll study negromancy but I'll be reveng'd!

GUIDO

Gentlemen, leave these dissensions;
Signior Rogero, you are a man of worth.

CLARIDIANA

True, all the city points at him for a knave.

GUIDO

You are of like reputation, Signior Claridiana.
The hatred 'twixt your grandsires first began;
Impute it to the folly of that age:
These your dissensions may erect a faction
Like to the Capulets and the Montagues.

MENDOZA

Put it to equal arbitration, choose your friends;
The senators will think 'em happy in 't.

ROGERO

I'll ne'er embrace the smoke of a furnace, the quintessence of mineral or simples, or, as I may say more learnedly, nor the spirit of quicksilver.

CLARIDIANA

Nor I, such a Centaur,—half a man, half an ass, and all a Jew!

GUIDO

Nay, then, we will be constables, and force a quiet. Gentlemen, keep 'em asunder, and help to persuade 'em.

[Exeunt at one door **MIZALDUS** and **CLARIDIANA**; at another **GUIDO** and **ROGERO**.

MENDOZA
Well, ladies, your husbands behave 'em as lustily on their wedding-days as e'er I heard any. Nay, lady-widow, you and I must have a falling; you're of Signior Mizaldus' faction, and I am your vowed enemy, from the bodkin to the pincase. Hark in your ear.

ABIGAIL
Well, Thais. O you're a cunning carver; we two, that any time these fourteen years have called sisters, brought and bred up together, that have told one another all our wanton dreams, talk'd all night long of young men, and spent many an idle hour; fasted upon the stones on St. Agnes' night together, practised all the petulant amorousness that delights young maids, yet have you conceal'd not only the marriage, but the man: and well you might deceive me, for I'll be sworn you never dream'd of him, and it stands against all reason you should enjoy him you never dream'd of.

THAIS
Is not all this the same in you? Did you ever manifest your sweetheart's nose, that I might nose him by't? commended his calf or his nether lip? apparent signs that you were not in love, or wisely covered it. Have you ever said, such a man goes upright, or has a better gait than any of the rest, as indeed, since he is proved a magnifico, I thought thou would'st have put it into my hands whate'er 't had been.

ABIGAIL
Well, wench, we have cross fates; our husbands such inveterate foes, and we such entire friends; but the best is we are neighbours, and our back arbors may afford visitation freely. Prithee, let us maintain our familiarity still, whatsoever thy husband do unto thee, as I am afraid he will cross it i' the nick.

THAIS
Faith, you little one, if I please him in one thing, he shall please me in all, that's certain. Who shall I have to keep my counsel if I miss thee? who shall teach me to use the bridle when the reins are in mine own hand? what to long for? when to take physic? where to be melancholy? Why, we two are one another's grounds, without which would be no music.

ABIGAIL
Well said, wench; and the prick-song we use shall be our husbands.

THAIS
I will long for swine's-flesh o' the first child.

ABIGAIL
Wilt 'ou, little Jew? And I to kiss thy husband upon the least belly-ache. This will mad 'em.

THAIS
I kiss thee, wench, for that, and with it confirm our friendship.

MENDOZA
By these sweet lips, widow!

LADY LENTULUS

Good my lord, learn to swear by rote;
Your birth and fortune makes my brain suppose
That, like a man heated with wines and lust,
She that is next your object is your mate,
Till the foul water have quench'd out the fire.
You, the duke's kinsman, tell me I am young,
Fair, rich, and virtuous. I myself will flatter
Myself, till you are gone that are more fair,
More rich, more virtuous, and more debonair:
All which are ladders to an higher reach.
Who drinks a puddle that may taste a spring?
Who kiss a subject that may hug a king?

MENDOZA
Yes, the camel always drinks in puddle-water;
And as for huggings, read antiquities.
Faith, madam, I'll board thee one of these days.

LADY LENTULUS
Ay, but ne'er bed me, my lord. My vow is firm,
Since God hath called me to this noble state,
Much to my grief, of virtuous widow-hood,
No man shall ever come within my gates.

MENDOZA
Wilt thou ram up thy porch-hold? O widow, I perceive
You're ignorant of the lover's legerdemain!
There is a fellow that by magic will assist
To murder princes invisible; I can command his spirit.
Or what say you to a fine scaling-ladder of ropes?
I can tell you I am a mad wag-halter;
But by the virtue I see seated in you,
And by the worthy fame is blazon'd of you;
By little Cupid, that is mighty nam'd,
And can command my looser follies down,
I love, and must enjoy, yet with such limits
As one that knows enforcèd marriage
To be the Furies' sister. Think of me.

ABIGAIL and **THAIS**
Ha, ha, ha!

MENDOZA
How now, lady? does the toy take you, as they say?

ABIGAIL
No, my lord; nor do we take your toy, as they say.
This is a child's birth that must not be delivered before a man,

Though your lordship might be a midwife for your chin.

MENDOZA
Some bawdy riddle, is 't not? You long till 't be night.

THAIS
No, my lord, women's longing comes after their marriage night. Sister, see you be constant now.

ABIGAIL
Why, dost think I'll make my husband a cuckold?
O here they come!

[Enter at several doors **MIZALDUS** with **CLARIDIANA**; **GUIDO**, with **ROGERO**, at another door; **MENDOZA** meets them.

MENDOZA
Signior Rogero, are you yet qualified?

ROGERO
Yes; does any man think I'll go like a sheep to the slaughter? Hands off, my lord; your lordship may chance come under my hands. If you do, I shall show myself a citizen, and revenge basely.

CLARIDIANA
I think, if I were receiving the Holy Sacrament,
His sight would make me gnash my teeth terribly.
But there's the beauty without parallel,
In whom the Graces and the Virtues meet!
In her aspect mild Honour sits and smiles;
And who looks there, were it the savage bear
But would derive new nature from her eyes?
But to be reconciled simply for him,
Were mankind to be lost again, I'd let it,
And a new heap of stones should stock the world.
In heaven and earth this power beauty hath—
It inflames temperance and temp'rates wrath.
Whate'er thou art, mine art thou, wise or chaste;
I shall set hard upon thy marriage-vow,
And write revenge high in thy husband's brow
In a strange character.—You may begin, sir.

MENDOZA
Signior Claridiana, I hope Signior Rogero thus employed me about a good office: 'twere worthy Cicero's tongue, a famous oration now; but friendship, that is mutually embraced of the gods,
And is Jove's usher to each sacred synod,
Without the which he could not reign in heaven,—
That over-goes my admiration, shall not
Under-go my censure!
These hot flames of rage, that else will be

As fire midst your nuptial jollity,
Burning the edge off from the present joy,
And keep you wake to terror.

CLARIDIANA
I have not yet swallowed the rhimatrix nor the onocentaur—the rhinoceros was monstrous!

GUIDO
Sir, be you of the more flexible nature, and confess an error.

CLARIDIANA
I must; the gods of love command,
And that bright star her eye, that guides my fate.—
Signior Rogero, joy, then, Signior Rogero!

ROGERO
Signior, sir? O devil!

THAIS
Good husband, show yourself a temperate man!
Your mother was a woman, I dare swear—
No tiger got you, nor no bear was rival
In your conception—you seem like the issue
The painters limn leaping from Envy's mouth,
That devours all he meets.

ROGERO
Had the last, or the least syllable
Of this more than immortal eloquence
Commenced to me when rage had been so high
Within my blood that it o'er-topt my soul,
Like to the lion when he hears the sound
Of Dian's bowstring in some shady wood,
I should have couch'd my lowly limb on earth
And held my silence a proud sacrifice.

CLARIDIANA
Slave, I will fight with thee at any odds;
Or name an instrument fit for destruction,
That e'er was made to make away a man,
I'll meet thee on the ridges of the Alps,
Or some inhospitable wilderness,
Stark-naked, at push of pike, or keen curtle-axe,
At Turkish sickle, Babylonian saw,
The ancient hooks of great Cadwallader,
Or any other heathen invention!

THAIS

O God bless the man!

LADY LENTULUS
Counsel him, good my lord!

MENDOZA
Our tongues are weary, and he desperate.
He does refuse to hear. What shall we do?

CLARIDIANA
I am not mad—I can hear, I can see, I can feel!
But a wise rage in man, wrong'd past compare,
Should be well nourish'd, as his virtues are.
I'd have it known unto each valiant sprite,
He wrongs no man that to himself does right.
Catzo, I ha' done; Signior Rogero, I ha' done!

GUIDO
By heaven!
This voluntary reconciliation, made
Freely and of itself, argues unfeign'd
And virtuous knot of love. So, sirs, embrace!

ROGERO
Sir, by the conscience of a Catholic man,
And by our mother Church, that binds
And doth atone in amity with God
The souls of men, that they with men be one,
I tread into the centre all the thoughts
Of ill in me toward you, and memory
Of what from you might aught disparage me;
Wishing unfeignedly it may sink low,
And, as untimely births, want power to grow.

MENDOZA
Christianly said! Signior, what would you have more?

CLARIDIANA
And so I swear. You're honest, onocentaur!

GUIDO
Nay, see now! Fie upon your turbulent spirit!
Did he doo 't in this form?

CLARIDIANA
If you think not this sufficient, you shall command me to be reconciled in another form—as a rhimatrix
or a rhinoceros.

MENDOZA
'Sblood! what will you do?

CLARIDIANA [To **THAIS**]
Well, give me your hands first: I am friends with you, i'faith. Thereupon I embrace you, kiss your wife, and God give us joy!

THAIS
You mean me and my husband?

CLARIDIANA
You take the meaning better than the speech, lady.

ROGERO
The like wish I, but ne'er can be the like,
And therefore wish I thee.

CLARIDIANA
By this bright light, that is deriv'd from thee——

THAIS
So, sir, you make me a very light creature!

CLARIDIANA
But that thou art a blessèd angel, sent
Down from the gods t' atone mortal men,
I would have thought deeds beyond all men's thoughts,
And executed more upon his corps.
O let him thank the beauty of this eye,
And not his resolute swords or destiny.

GUIDO
What say'st thou, Mizaldus? Come, applaud this jubilee,
A day these hundred years before not truly known
To these divided factions.

CLARIDIANA
No, nor this day had it been falsely born,
But that I mean to sound it with his horn.

MIZALDUS
I liked the former jar better. Then they show'd like men and soldiers, now like cowards and lechers.

GUIDO
Well said, Mizaldus; thou art like the bass viol in a consort,—let the other instruments wish and delight in your highest sense, thou art still grumbling.

CLARIDIANA

Nay, sweet, receive it

[Gives a letter to **THAIS**.

—and in it my heart:
And when thou read'st a moving syllable,
Think that my soul was secretary to 't.
It is your love, and not the odious wish
Of my revenge in styling him a cuckold,
Makes me presume thus far. Then read it, fair,
My passion's ample, as your beauties are.

THAIS
Well, sir, we will not stick with you.

GUIDO
And, gentlemen, since it hath hapt so fortunately,
I do entreat we may all meet to-morrow
In some heroic masque, to grace the nuptials
Of the most noble Count of Cyprus.

MENDOZA
Who does the young count marry?

GUIDO
O, sir,
Who but the very heir of all her sex,
That bears the palm of beauty from 'em all?
Others, compared to her, show like faint stars
To the full moon of wonder in her face:—
The Lady Isabella, the late widow
To the deceased and noble Viscount Hermus.

MENDOZA
Law you there, widow, there's one of the last edition,
Whose husband yet retains in his cold trunk
Some little airing of his noble guest;
Yet she a fresh bride as the month of May.

LADY LENTULUS
Well, my lord, I am none of these
That have my second husband bespoke;
My door shall be a testimony of it;
And but these noble marriages incite me,
My much abstracted presence should have show'd it.
If you come to me, hark in your ear, my lord,
Look your ladder of ropes be strong,
For I shall tie you to your tackling.

GUIDO
Gentlemen, your answer to the masque.

OMNES
Your honour leads: we'll follow.

ROGERO
Signior Claridiana.

CLARIDIANA
I attend you, sir.

Tha.
You'll be constant?

[Exeunt **ALL** but **CLARIDIANA**.

CLARIDIANA
Above the adamant; the goat's blood shall not break me.
Yet shallow fools and plainer moral men,
That understand not what they undertake,
Fall in their own snares or come short of vengeance.
No; let the sun view with an open face,
And afterward shrink in his blushing cheeks,
Ashamed and cursing of the fix'd decree,
That makes his light bawd to the crimes of men.
When I have ended what I now devise,
Apollo's oracle shall swear me wise.
Strumpet his wife! branch my false-seeming friend!
And make him foster what my hate begot,
A bastard, that, when age and sickness seize him,
Shall be a corsive to his griping heart.
I'll write to her; for what her modesty
Will not permit, nor my adulterate forcing,
That blushless herald shall not fear to tell.
Rogero shall know yet that his foe's a man,
And, what is more, a true Italian!

[Exit.

ACT II

SCENE I

Venice.—Hall in Roberto's house.

Enter **ROBERTO, LORD CARDINAL, ISABELLA, LADY LENTULUS, ABIGAIL**, and **THAIS**. Lights.

ROBERTO
My grave Lord Cardinal, we congratulate,
And zealously do entertain your love,
That from your high and divine contemplation
You have vouchsafed to consummate a day
Due to our nuptials. O may this knot you knit—
This individual Gordian grasp of hands,
In sight of God so fairly intermixt—
Never be sever'd, as Heaven smiles at it,
By all the darts shot by infernal Jove!
Angels of grace, Amen, Amen, say to 't!
Fair lady-widow, and my worthy mistress,
Do you keep silence for a wager?

THAIS
Do you ask a woman that question, my lord, when she enforcedly pursues what she's forbidden? I think, if I had been tied to silence, I should have been worthy the cucking-stool ere this time.

ROBERTO
You shall not be my orator, lady, that pleads thus for your self.

[Enter a **SERVANT**.

SERVANT
My lord, the masquers are at hand.

ROBERTO
Give them kind entertainment.—Some worthy friends of mine, my lord, unknown to me, too lavish of their loves, bring their own welcome in a solemn masque.

ABIGAIL
I am glad there's noblemen in the masque, with our husbands to overrule them; they had shamed us all else.

THAIS
Why? for why, I pray?

ABIGAIL
Why?—marry, they had come in with some city show else; hired a few tinsel coats, at the vizard-makers, which would ha' made them look for all the world like bakers in their linen bases and mealy vizards, new come from boulting. I saw a show once at the marriage of Magnificero's daughter, presented by Time, which Time was an old bald thing, a servant: 'twas the best man; he was a dyer, and came in likeness of the rainbow, in all manner of colours, to show his art; but the rainbow smelt of urine so we were all afraid the property was changed, and look'd for a shower. Then came in after him, one that, it seem'd, feared no colours—a grocer that had trimm'd up himself handsomely: he was justice, and show'd

reasons why. And I think this grocer—I mean this justice—had borrowed a weather-beaten balance from some justice of a conduit, both which scales were replenish'd with the choice of his ware. And the more liberally to show his nature, he gave every woman in the room her handful.

THAIS
O great act of justice! Well, and my husband come cleanly off with this, he shall ne'er betray his weakness more, but confess himself a citizen hereafter, and acknowledge their wit, for alas! they come short.

[Enter in the Masque, the **COUNT OF MASSINO**, **MENDOZA**, **CLARIDIANA**, and **TORCH-BEARERS**. They deliver their shields to their several mistresses—that is to say, **MENDOZA** to the **LADY LENTULUS**; **CLARIDIANA** to **THAIS**; to **ISABELLA**, **MASSINO**; to **ABIGAIL**, **ROGERO**.

ISABELLA
Good my lord, be my expositor.

[To the **CARDINAL**.

CARDINAL
The sun setting, a man pointing at it:
The motto, Senso tamen ipse calorem.
Fair bride, some servant of yours, that here imitates
To have felt the heat of love bred in your brightness,
But setting thus from him by marriage;
He only here acknowledgeth your power,
And must expect beams of a morrow-sun.

LADY LENTULUS
Lord Bridegroom, will you interpret me?

ROBERTO
A sable shield: the word, Vidua spes.
What—the forlorn hope, in black, despairing?
Lady Lentulus, is this the badge of all your suitors?

LADY LENTULUS
Ay, by my troth, my lord, if they come to me.

ROBERTO
I could give it another interpretation. Methinks this lover has learn'd of women to deal by contraries; if so, then here he says, the widow is his only hope.

LADY LENTULUS
No; good my lord, let the first stand.

ROBERTO
Inquire of him, and he'll resolve the doubt.

ABIGAIL
What's here?—a ship sailing nigh her haven?
With good ware belike: 'tis well ballast.

THAIS
O this your device smells of the merchant. What's your ship's name, I pray? The Forlorn Hope?

ABIGAIL
No; The Merchant Royal.

THAIS
And why not Adventurer?

ABIGAIL
You see no likelihood of that: would it not fain be in the haven? The word, Ut tangerem portum. Marry, for aught I know; God grant it. What's there?

THAIS
Mine's an azure shield: marry, what else? I should tell thee more than I understand; but the word is, Aut pretio, aut precibus.

ABIGAIL
Ay, ay, some common-council device.

[They take the **WOMEN**, and dance the first change.

MENDOZA
Fair widow, how like you this change?

LADY LENTULUS
I chang'd too lately to like any.

MENDOZA
O your husband! you wear his memory like a death's-head.
For Heaven's love, think of me as of the man
Whose dancing days you see are not yet done.

LADY LENTULUS
Yet you sink a-pace, sir.

MENDOZA
The fault's in my upholsterer, lady.

ROGERO
Thou shalt as soon find Truth telling a lie,
Virtue a bawd, Honesty a courtier,
As me turn'd recreant to thy least design.
Love makes me speak, and he makes love divine.

ABIGAIL

Would Love could make you so! but 'tis his guise
To let us surfeit ere he ope our eyes.

THAIS

You grasp my hand too hard, i'faith, fair sir.

[**CLARIDIANA** holds her by the hand.

CLARIDIANA

Not as you grasp my heart, unwilling wanton.
Were but my breast bare and anatomised,
Thou shouldst behold there how thou torturest it;
And as Apelles limn'd the Queen of Love,
In her right hand grasping a heart in flames,
So may I thee, fairer, but crueller.

THAIS

Well, sir, your vizor gives you colour for what you say.

CLARIDIANA

Grace me to wear this favour; 'tis a gem
That vails to your eyes, though not to the eagle's,
And in exchange give me one word of comfort.

THAIS

Ay, marry: I like this wooer well:
He'll win's pleasure out o' the stones.

[The second change, **ISABELLA** falls in love with **MASSINO**; when they change she speaks.

ISABELLA

Change is no robbery; yet in this change
Thou robb'st me of my heart. Sure Cupid's here,
Disguisèd like a pretty torch-bearer,
And makes his brand a torch, that with more sleight
He may entrap weak women. Here the sparks
Fly, as in Ætna from his father's anvil.
O powerful boy!
My heart's on fire, and unto mine eyes
The raging flames ascend like to two beacons,
Summoning my strongest powers; but all too late;
The conqueror already opes the gate.
I will not ask his name.

ABIGAIL

You dare put it into my hands.

ROGERO
Zounds, do you think I will not?

ABIGAIL
Then thus: to-morrow (you'll be secret, servant)—

ROGERO
All that I do, I'll do in secret.

ABIGAIL
My husband goes to Maurano to renew the farm he has.

ROGERO
Well, what time goes the jakes-farmer?

ABIGAIL
He shall not be long out, but you shall put in, I warrant you. Have a care that you stand just i' the nick about six o'clock in the evening; my maid shall conduct you up. To save mine honour, you must come up darkling, and to avoid suspicion.

ROGERO
Zounds! hoodwink'd! and if you'll open all, sweet lady——

ABIGAIL
But if you fail to do 't—

ROGERO
The sun shall fail the day first.

ABIGAIL
Tie this ring fast, you may be sure to know.
You'll brag of this, now you have brought me to the bay.

ROGERO
Pox o' this masque! would 'twere done! I might
To my apothecary's for some stirring meats!

THAIS
Methinks, sir, you should blush e'en through your vizor.
I have scarce patience to dance out the rest.

CLARIDIANA
The worse my fate, that ploughs a marble quarry:
Pygmalion, yet thy image was more kind,
Although thy love not half so true as mine.
Dance they that list, I sail against the wind.

THAIS
Nay, sir, betray not your infirmities,
You'll make my husband jealous by and by.
We will think of you, and that presently.

MASSINO
The spheres ne'er danced unto a better tune.
Sound music there!

[The third change ended, **LADIES** fall off.

ISABELLA
'Twas music that he spake.

ROBERTO
Gallants, I thank you, and begin a health
To your mistresses!
Three or four. Fair thanks, Sir Bridegroom.

ISABELLA [Aside]
He speaks not to this pledge; has he no mistress?
Would I might choose one for him! but 't may be
He doth adore a brighter star than we.

ROBERTO
Sit, ladies, sit; you have had standing long.

[**MASSINO** dances a Levalto or a Galliard, and in the midst of it falleth into the Bride's lap, but straight leaps up and danceth it out.

MENDOZA
Bless the man! sprightly and nobly done!

THAIS
What, is your ladyship hurt?

ISABELLA
O no, an easy fall.
[Aside]
Was I not deep enough, thou god of lust,
But I must further wade! I am his now,
As sure as Juno's Jove's! Hymen, take flight,
And see not me, 'tis not my wedding night.

[Exit **ISABELLA**.

CARDINAL
The bride's departed, discontent it seems.

ROBERTO
We'll after her. Gallants, unmasque I pray,
And taste a homely banquet, we entreat.

[Exeunt **ROBERTO**, **CARDINAL**, and lights.

CLARIDIANA
Candied eringoes, I beseech thee.

MENDOZA
Come, widow, I'll be bold to put you in.
My lord, will you have a sociate?

[Exeunt **THAIS**, **LADY LENTULUS**, **ABIGAIL**, and **MENDOZA**.

MASSINO
Good gentlemen, if I have any interest in you,
Let me depart unknown; 'tis a disgrace
Of an eternal memory.

ROGERO
What, the fall, my lord?—as common a thing as can be. The stiffest man in Italy may fall between a woman's legs.

CLARIDIANA
Would I had changed places with you, my lord—would it had been my hap!

MASSINO
What cuckold laid his horns in my way?
Signior Claridiana, you were by the lady when I fell:
Do you think I hurt her?

CLARIDIANA
You could not hurt her, my lord, between the legs.

MASSINO
What was 't I fell withal?

ROGERO
A cross-point, my lord.

MASSINO
Cross-point, indeed.
Well, if you love me, let me hence unknown;
The silence yours, the disgrace mine own.

[Exeunt **CLARIDIANA** and **ROGERO**.

[Enter **ISABELLA** with a gilt goblet, and meets **MASSINO**.

ISABELLA
Sir, if wine were nectar, I'd begin a health
To her that were most gracious in your eye:
Yet deign, as simply 'tis the gift of Bacchus,
To give her pledge that drinks. This god of wine
Cannot inflame me more to appetite,
Though he be co-supreme with mighty Love,
Than thy fair shape.

MASSINO
Zounds! she comes to deride me.

ISABELLA
That kiss shall serve
To be a pledge, although my lips should starve.—
[Aside]
No trick to get that vizor from his face?

MASSINO
I will steal hence, and so conceal disgrace.

ISABELLA
Sir, have you left naught behind?

MASSINO
Yes, Lady, but the fates will not permit
(As gems once lost are seldom or never found)
I should convey it with me. Sweet, good-night!
[Aside]
She bends to me: there's my fall again.

[Exit.

ISABELLA
He's gone! That lightning that a while doth strike
Our eyes with amaz'd brightness, and on a sudden
Leaves us in prison'd darkness! Lust, thou art high;
My similes may well come from the sky.
Anna, Anna!

[Enter **ANNA**.

ANNA
Madam, did you call?

ISABELLA
Follow yond stranger; prithee learn his name.
We may hereafter thank him.

[Exit **ANNA**.

How I dote!
Is he not a god
That can command what other men would win
With the hard'st advantage? I must have him,
Or, shadow-like, follow his fleeting steps.
Were I as Daphne, and he followed chase,
(Though I rejected young Apollo's love,
And like a dream beguile his wand'ring steps;)
Should he pursue me through the neighbouring grove,
Each cowslip-stalk should trip a willing fall,
Till he were mine, who till then am his thrall.
Nor will I blush, since worthy is my chance:
'Tis said that Venus with a satyr slept;
And how much short came she of my fair aim!
Then, Queen of Love, a precedent I'll be,
To teach fair women learn to love of me.
Speak, music: what's his name?

[Enter **ANNA**.

ANNA
Madam, it was the worthy Count Massino.

ISABELLA
Blest be thy tongue! The worthy count indeed,
The worthiest of the worthies. Trusty Anna,
Hast thou pack'd up those monies, plate, and jewels
I gave direction for?

ANNA
Yes, madam; I have truss'd up them, that many a proper man has been truss'd up for.

ISABELLA
I thank thee. Take the wings of night,
Beloved secretary, and post with them to Pavia;
There furnish up some stately palace
Worthy to entertain the king of love:
Prepare it for my coming and my love's.
Ere Phœbus' steeds once more unharness'd be,
Or ere he sport with his belovèd Thetis,
The silver-footed goddess of the sea,
We will set forward. Fly like the northern wind,

Or swifter, Anna,—fleet like to my mind.

ANNA
I am just of your mind, madam. I am gone.

[Exit **ANNA**.

ISABELLA
So to the house of death the mourner goes,
That is bereft of what his soul desired,
As I to bed—I to my nuptial bed,
The heaven on earth: so to thought-slaughters went
The pale Andromeda, bedew'd with tears.
When every minute she expected gripes
Of a fell monster, and in vain bewail'd
The act of her creation. Sullen Night,
That look'st with sunk eyes on my nuptial bed,
With ne'er a star that smiles upon the end,
Mend thy slack pace, and lend the malcontent,
The hoping lover, and the wishing bride,
Beams that too long thou shadowest: or, if not,
In spite of thy fix'd front, when my loath'd mate
Shall struggle in due pleasure for his right,
I'll think 't my love, and die in that delight!

[Exit.

SCENE II

Venice.—A street.

Enter at several doors **ABIGAIL** and **THAIS**.

ABIGAIL
Thais, you're an early riser. I have that to show will make your hair stand an-end.

THAIS
Well, lady, and I have that to show you will bring your courage down. What would you say and I would name a party saw your husband court, kiss, nay, almost go through for the hole?

ABIGAIL
How, how? what would I say? nay, by this light! what would I not do? If ever Amazon fought better, or more at the face than I'll do, let me never be thought a new married wife. Come, unmask her; 'tis some admirable creature, whose beauty you need not paint; I warrant you, 'tis done to your hand.

THAIS

Would any woman but I be abused to her face? Prithee read the contents. Know'st thou the character?

ABIGAIL

'Tis my husband's hand, and a love-letter; but for the contents I find none in it. Has the lustful monster, all back and belly, starved me thus? What defect does he see in me? I'll be sworn, wench, I am of as pliant and yielding a body to him, e'en which way he will—he may turn me as he list himself. What? and dedicate to thee! Ay, marry, here's a stile so high as a man cannot help a dog o'er it. He was wont to write to me in the city-phrase, My good Abigail. Here's astonishment of nature, unparallel'd excellency, and most unequal rarity of creation!—three such words will turn any honest woman in the world whore; for a woman is never won till she know not what to answer; and beshrew me if I understand any of these. You are the party, I perceive, and here's a white sheet, that your husband has promis'd me to do penance in: you must not think to dance the shaking of the sheets alone; though there be not such rare phrases in 't, 'tis more to the matter: a legible hand, but for the dash or the (he) and (as): short bawdy parentheses as ever you saw, to the purpose; he has not left out a prick, I warrant you, wherein he has promis'd to do me any good; but the law's in mine own hand.

THAIS

I ever thought by his red beard he would prove a Judas; here am I bought and sold; he makes much of me indeed. Well, wench, we were best wisely in time seek for prevention; I should be loath to take drink and die on 't, as I am afraid I shall, that he will lie with thee.

ABIGAIL

To be short, sweetheart, I'll be true to thee, though a liar to my husband. I have signed your husband's bill like a woodcock, as he is held; persuaded him (since naught but my love can assuage his violent passions) he should enjoy, like a private friend, the pleasures of my bed. I told him my husband was to go to Maurano to-day, to renew a farm he has; and in the meantime he might be tenant at will to use mine. This false fire has so took with him, that he's ravish'd afore he come. I have had stones on him all red. Dost know this?

THAIS

Ay, too well; it blushes, for his master.

[Points to the ring.

ABIGAIL

Now my husband will be hawking about thee anon, and thou canst meet him closely.

THAIS

By my faith, I would be loth in the dark, and he knew me.

ABIGAIL

I mean thus: the same occasion will serve him too; they are birds of a feather, and will fly together, I warrant thee, wench; appoint him to come; say that thy husband's gone for Maurano, and tell me anon if thou madest not his heart-blood spring for joy in his face.

THAIS

I conceive you not all this while.

ABIGAIL

Then th' art a barren woman, and no marvel if thy husband love thee not. The hour for both to come is six—a dark time fit for purblind lovers; and with cleanly conveyance by the nigglers our maids, they shall be translated into our bed-chambers. Your husband into mine, and mine into yours.

THAIS

But you mean they shall come in at the backdoors?

ABIGAIL

Who? our husbands? nay, an' they come not in at the fore-doors there will be no pleasure in 't. But we two will climb over our garden-pales, and come in that way (the chastest that are in Venice will stray for a good turn), and thus wittily will we be stowed—you into my house to your husband, and I into your house to my husband; and I warrant thee before a month come to an end, they'll crack louder of this night's lodging than the bedsteads.

THAIS

All is if our maids keep secret.

ABIGAIL

Mine is a maid I'll be sworn; she has kept her secrets hitherto.

THAIS

Troth, and I never had any sea-captain boarded in my house.

ABIGAIL

Go to, then; and the better to avoid suspicion, thus we must insist: they must come up darkling, recreate themselves with their delight an hour or two, and after a million kisses or so—

THAIS

But is my husband content to come darkling?

ABIGAIL

What, not to save mine honour? He that will run through fire, as he has profess'd, will, by the heat of his love, grope in the dark! I warrant him he shall save mine honour.

THAIS

I am afraid my voice will discover me.

ABIGAIL

Why, then, you're best say nothing, and take it thus quietly when your husband comes.

THAIS

Ay, but you know a woman cannot choose but speak in these cases.

ABIGAIL

Bite in your nether-lip, and I warrant you;
Or make as if you were whiffing tobacco;
Or puich like me. Gods so! I hear thy husband!

[Exit **ABIGAIL**.

THAIS
Farewell, wise woman.

[Enter **ROGERO**.

ROGERO
Now 'gins my vengeance mount high in my lust:
'Tis a rare creature, she'll do 't i'faith;
And I am arm'd at all points. A rare whiblin,
To be revenged, and yet gain pleasure in 't,
One height above revenge! Yet what a slave am I!
Are there not younger brothers enough, but we must
Branch one another? O but mine's revenge!
And who on that does dream
Must be a tyrant ever in extreme.—
O my wife Thais, get my breakfast ready;
I must into the country to my farm I have
Some two miles off, and, as I think,
Shall not come home to-night. Jaques, Jaques?
Get my vessel ready to row me down the river.
Prithee make haste, sweet girl.

[Exit **ROGERO**.

THAIS
So, there's one fool shipp'd away. Are your cross-points discovered? Get your breakfast ready! By this light I'll tie you to hard fare; I have been too sparing of that you prodigally offer voluntary to another: well, you will be a tame fool hereafter,
The finest light is when we first defraud;
Husband, to-night 'tis I must lie abroad.

[Exit.

SCENE III

Venice.—Roberto's house.

Enter **ISABELLA**, and a **PAGE** with a letter.

ISABELLA
Here, take this letter, bear it to the count.
But, boy, first tell, think'st thou I am in love?

PAGE
Madam, I cannot tell.

ISABELLA
Canst thou not tell? Dost thou not see my face?
Is not the face the index of the mind?
And canst thou not distinguish love by that?

PAGE
No, madam.

ISABELLA
Then take this letter and deliver it
Unto the worthy count. No, fie upon him!
Come back: tell me, why shouldst thou think
That same's a love-letter?

PAGE
I do not think so, madam.

ISABELLA
I know thou dost; for thou dost ever use
To hold the wrong opinion. Tell me true,
Dost thou not think that letter is of love?

PAGE
If you would have me think so, madam, yes.

ISABELLA
What, dost thou think thy lady is so fond?
Give me the letter; thyself shall see it.
Yet I should tear it in the breaking ope,
And make him lay a wrongful charge on thee,
And say thou brokest it open by the way,
And saw what heinous things I charge him with.
But 'tis all one, the letter is not of love;
Therefore deliver it unto himself,
And tell him he's deceived—I do not love him.
But if he think so, bid him come to me,
And I'll confute him straight: I'll show him reasons—
I'll show him plainly why I cannot love him.
And if he hap to read it in thy hearing,
Or chance to tell thee that the words were sweet,
Do not thou then disclose my lewd intent
Under those siren words, and how I mean
To use him when I have him at my will;
For then thou wilt destroy the plot that's laid,
And make him fear to yield when I do wish

Only to have him yield; for when I have him,
None but myself shall know how I will use him.
Begone! why stayest thou?—yet return again.

PAGE
Ay, madam.

ISABELLA
Why dost thou come again? I bade thee go.
If I say go, never return again.

[Exit **PAGE**.

My blood, like to a troubled ocean,
Cuff'd with the winds, incertain where to rest,
Butts at the utmost shore of every limb!
My husband's not the man I would have had.
O my new thoughts to this brave sprightly lord
Was fix'd to by? that hid fire lovers feel!
Where was my mind before—that refined judgment
That represents rare objects to our passions?
Or did my lust beguile me of my sense,
Making me feast upon such dangerous cates,
For present want, that needs must breed a surfeit?
How was I shipwrack'd? Yet, Isabella, think;
Thy husband is a noble gentleman,
Young, wise, and rich; think what fate follows thee,
And naught but lust doth blind thy worthy love.
I will desist. O no, it may not be.
Even as a headstrong courser bears away
His rider, vainly striving him to stay;
Or as a sudden gale thrusts into sea
The haven-touching bark, now near the lea,
So wavering Cupid brings me back amain,
And purple Love resumes his darts again:
Here of themselves, thy shafts come as if shot,
Better than I thy quiver knows 'em not.

[Enter **COUNT MASSINO** and the **PAGE**.

PAGE
Madam, the count.

MASSINO
So fell the Trojan wanderer on the Greek,
And bore away his ravish'd prize to Troy.
For such a beauty, brighter than his Danae,
Jove should (methinks) now come himself again.

Lovely Isabella, I confess me mortal—
Not worthy to serve thee in thought, I swear;
Yet shall not this same overflow of favour
Diminish my vow'd duty to your beauty.

ISABELLA
Your love, my lord, I blushingly proclaim it,
Hath power to draw me through a wilderness,
Were 't armed with furies, as with furious beasts.
Boy, bid our train be ready; we'll to horse.

[Exit **PAGE**.

My lord, I should say something, but I blush;
Courting is not befitting to our sex.

MASSINO
I'll teach you how to woo. Say you have loved me long,
And tell me that a woman's feeble tongue
Was never tuned unto a wooing-string;
Yet for my sake you will forget your sex,
And court my love with strain'd immodesty:
Then bid me make you happy with a kiss.

ISABELLA
Sir, though women do not woo, yet for your sake
I am content to leave that civil custom,
And pray you kiss me.

MASSINO
Now use some unexpected ambages
To draw me further into Vulcan's net.

ISABELLA
You love not me so well as I love you.

MASSINO
Fair lady, but I do.

ISABELLA
Then show your love.

MASSINO
Why, in this kiss I show 't, and in my vowed service
This wooing shall suffice: 'tis easier far
To make the current of a silver brook
Convert his flowing backward to his spring
Than turn a woman wooer. There's no cause

Can turn the settled course of Nature's laws.

ISABELLA
My lord, will you pursue the plot?

MASSINO
The letter gives direction here for Pavy.
To horse, to horse! Thus on Eurydice,
With looks regardiant, did the Thracian gaze,
And lost his gift while he desired the sight:
But wiser I, led by more powerful charm,
I'd see the world win thee from out mine arm.

[Exeunt.

SCENE IV

Venice.—Courtyard of Robert's house.

[Enter at several doors **CLARIDIANA** and **GUIDO**.

GUIDO
Zounds! is the hurricano coming? Claridiana, what's the matter?

[A trampling of horses heard.

CLARIDIANA
The Countess of Suevia has new taken horse.—
Fly, Phœbus, fly, the hour is six o'clock!

GUIDO
Whither is she gone, signior?

CLARIDIANA
Even as Jove went to meet his Semele—
To the devil, I think.

GUIDO
You know not wherefore?

CLARIDIANA
To say sooth. I do not.—
So in immortal wise shall I arrive——

GUIDO
At the gallows. What, in a passion, signior?

CLARIDIANA
Zounds! do not hold me, sir.—
Beauteous Thais, I am all thine wholly.
The staff is now advancing for the rest,
And when I tilt, Rogero, 'ware thy crest!

[Exit **CLARIDIANA**.

GUIDO
What's here?
The cap'ring god-head tilting in the air?

[Enter **ROBERTO** in his night-gown and cap, with **SERVANTS**; he kneels down.

ROBERTO
The gods send her remorse, a poor old age,
Eternal woe, and sickness' lasting rage!

GUIDO
My lord, you may yet o'ertake 'em.

ROBERTO
Furies supply that place, for I will not! No:
She can forsake me when pleasure's in the full,
Fresh and untired;
What would she on the least barren coldness?
I warrant you she has already got
Her bravoes and her ruffians; the meanest whore
Will have one buckler, but your great ones more.
The shores of Sicil retain not such a monster,
Though to galley-slaves they daily prostitute.
To let the nuptial tapers give light to her new lust!
Who would have thought it? She that could no more
Forsake my company than can the day
Forsake the glorious presence of the sun!—
When I was absent then her gallèd eyes
Would have shed April showers, and outwept
The clouds in that same o'er-passionate mood,
When they drowned all the world, yet now forsakes me!
Women, your eyes shed glances like the sun:
Now shines your brightness, now your light is done.
On the sweetest flowers you shine—'tis but by chance,
And on the basest weed you'll waste a glance.
Your beams, once lost, can never more be found,
Unless we wait until your course run round,
And take you at fifth hand. Since I cannot
Enjoy the noble title of a man,

But after-ages, as our virtues are
Buried whilst we are living, will sound out
My infamy and her degenerate shame,
Yet in my life I'll smother 't, if I may,
And like a dead man to the world bequeath
These houses of vanity, mills, and lands.
Take what you will, I will not keep, among you, servants:
And welcome some religious monastery.
A true sworn beads-man I'll hereafter be,
And wake the morning cock with holy prayers.

SERVANT
Good my lord—noble master—

ROBERTO
Dissuade me not, my will shall be my king;
I thank thee, wife; a fair change thou has given;
I leave thy lust to woo the love of Heaven!

[Exit cum servis.

GUIDO
This is conversion, is 't not—as good as might have been? He turns religious upon his wife's turning courtesan. This is just like some of our gallant prodigals, when they have consum'd their patrimonies wrongfully, they turn Capuchins for devotion.

[Exit.

ACT III

SCENE I

Venice.—Outside Lady Lentulus' house.

CLARIDIANA and **ROGERO**, being in a readiness, are received in at one another's houses by their **MAIDS**.

[Then enter **MENDOZA**, with a **PAGE**, to the Lady Lentulus' window.

MENDOZA
Night, like a solemn mourner, frowns on earth,
Envying that day should force her doff her robes,
Or Phœbus chase away her melancholy.
Heaven's eyes look faintly through her sable masque,
And silver Cynthia hides her in her sphere,
Scorning to grace black Night's solemnity.
Be unpropitious, Night, to villain thoughts,

But let thy diamonds shine on virtuous love.
This is the lower house of high-built heaven,
Where my chaste Phœbe sits inthroned 'mong thoughts
So purely good, brings her to heaven on earth.
Such power hath souls in contemplation!
Sing, boy (though night yet), like the morning's lark—

[Music plays.

A soul that's clear is light, though heaven be dark.
The Lady Lentulus at her window.

LADY LENTULUS
Who speaks in music to us?

MENDOZA
Sweet, 'tis I. Boy, leave me and to bed.

[Exit **PAGE**.

LADY LENTULUS
I thank you for your music; now, good-night.

MENDOZA
Leave not the world yet, Queen of Chastity;
Keep promise with thy love Endymion,
And let me meet thee there on Latmus' top.
'Tis I, whose virtuous hopes are firmly fix'd
On the fruition of thy chaste vow'd love.

LADY LENTULUS
My lord,
Your honour made me promise you ascent
Into my house, since my vow barr'd my doors,
By some wit's engine made for theft and lust;
Yet for your honour, and my humble fame,
Check your blood's passions, and return, dear lord.
Suspicion is a dog that still doth bite
Without a cause: this act gives food to envy;
Swoll'n big, it bursts, and poisons our clear flames.

MENDOZA
Envy is stingless when she looks on thee.

LADY LENTULUS
Envy is blind, my lord, and cannot see.

MENDOZA

If you break promise, fair, you break my heart.

LADY LENTULUS
Then come,—yet stay! ascend,—yet let us part.
I fear,—yet know not what I fear.
Your love is precious, yet mine honour's dear.

MENDOZA
If I do stain thy honour with foul lust,
May thunder strike me to show Jove is just!

LADY LENTULUS
Then come, my lord; on earth your vow is given.
This aid I'll lend you.

[He throws up a ladder of cords, which she makes fast to some part of the window; he ascends, and at top falls.

MENDOZA
Thus I mount my heaven:
Receive me, sweet!

LADY LENTULUS
O me, unhappy wretch!
How fares your honour? Speak, fate-cross'd lord!
If life retain his seat within you, speak!
Else like that Sestian dame, that saw her love
Cast by the frowning billows on the sands,
And lean death, swoll'n big with the Hellespont,
In bleak Leander's body—like his love,
Come I to thee. One grave shall serve us both!

MENDOZA
Stay, miracle of women! yet I breathe.
Though death be entered in this tower of flesh,
He is not conqueror; my heart stands out,
And yields to thee, scorning his tyranny!

LADY LENTULUS
My doors are vow'd shut, and I cannot help you.
Your wounds are mortal; wounded is mine honour
If there the town-guard find you. Unhappy dame!
Relief is perjur'd,—my vow kept, shame!
What hellish destiny did twist my fate!

MENDOZA
Rest seize thine eyelids; be not passionate;
Sweet, sleep secure; I'll remove myself,

That viper Envy shall not spot thy fame:
I'll take that poison with me, my soul's rest,
For like a serpent I'll creep on my breast.

LADY LENTULUS
Thou more than man! Love-wounded, joy and grief
Fight in my blood. Thy wounds and constancy
Are both so strong, none can have victory!

MENDOZA
Darken the world, earth's queen; get thee to bed;
The earth is light while those two stars are spread:
Their splendour will betray me to men's eyes.
Veil thy bright face; for if thou longer stay,
Phœbus will rise to thee and make night day.

LADY LENTULUS
To part and leave you hurt my soul doth fear.

MENDOZA
To part from hence I cannot, you being there.

LADY LENTULUS
We'll move together, then fate love controls;
And as we part, so bodies part from souls.

MENDOZA
Mine is the earth, thine the refinèd fire;
I am mortal, thou divine; then soul mount higher.

LADY LENTULUS
Why then, take comfort, sweet; I'll see you to-morrow.

MENDOZA
My wounds are nothing; thy loss breeds my sorrow.

[Exit **LADY LENTULUS**.

See now 'tis dark!
Support your master, legs, a little further;
Faint not, bold heart, with anguish of my wound;
Try further yet. Can blood weigh down my soul?
Desire is vain without ability.

[He staggers on, and then falls down.

Thus falls a monarch, if fate push at him.

[Enter a **CAPTAIN** and the **WATCH**.

CAPTAIN
Come on, my hearts; we are the city's security. I'll give you your charge, and then, like courtiers, every man spy out. Let no man in my company be afraid to speak to a cloak lined with velvet, nor tremble at the sound of a gingling spur.

WATCH
May I never be counted a cock of the game if I fear spurs, but be gelded like a capon for the preserving of my voice.

CAPTAIN
I'll have none of my band refrain to search a venereal house, though his wife's sister be a lodger there; nor take two shillings of the bawd to save the gentlemen's credits that are aloft, and so, like voluntary panders, leave them, to the shame of all halberdiers.

2ND WATCH
Nay, the wenches, we'll tickle them, that's flat.

CAPTAIN
If you meet a shevoiliero, that's in the gross phrase a knight that swaggers in the street, and, being taken, has no money in his purse to pay for his fees, it shall be a part of your duty to entreat me to let him go.

WATCH
O marvellous! is there such shevoiliers?

2ND WATCH
Some two hundred, that's the least, that are reveal'd.

[**MENDOZA** groans.

CAPTAIN
What groan is that? Bring a light. Who lies there?
It is the Lord Mendoza, kinsman to our duke.
Speak, good my lord: relate your dire mischance;
Life, like a fearful servant, flies his master;
Art must atone them, or th' whole man is lost.
Convey him to a surgeon's, then return;

[Part of the **WATCH** bear away **MENDOZA**.

No place shall be unsearch'd until we find
The truth of this mischance. Make haste again.
Whose house is this stands open? In and search
What guests that house contains, and bring them forth.

[Exit the **WATCH** to search the houses of Rogero and Claridiana.

This noble man's misfortune stirs my quiet,
And fills my soul with fearful fantasies;
But I'll unwind this labyrinth of doubt,
Else industry shall lose part of itself's labour.

[Re-enter the **WATCH** with **CLARIDIANA** and **ROGERO** taken in one another's houses in their shirts and night-gowns. They see one another.

Who have we there? Signiors, cannot you tell us
How our prince's kinsman came wounded to the death
Nigh to your houses?

ROGERO
Heyday! cross-ruff at midnight! Is't Christmas,
You go a-gaming to your neighbour's house?

CLARIDIANA
Dost make a mummer of me, ox-head?

CAPTAIN
Make answer, gentlemen, it doth concern you.

ROGERO
Ox-head will bear an action; I'll ha' the law; I'll not be yoked. Bear witness, gentlemen, he calls me ox-head.

CAPTAIN
Do you hear, sir?

CLARIDIANA
Very well, very well; take law and hang thyself; I care not. Had she no other but that good face to dote upon? I'd rather she had dealt with a dangerous Frenchman than with such a pagan.

CAPTAIN
Are you mad? Answer my demand.

ROGERO
I am as good a Christian as thyself,
Though my wife have now new christen'd me.

CAPTAIN
Are you deaf, you make no answer?

CLARIDIANA
Would I had had the circumcising of thee, Jew; I'd ha' cut short your cuckold-maker; I would i'faith, I would i'faith!

CAPTAIN
Away with them to prison! they'll answer better there.

ROGERO
Not too fast, gentlemen; what's our crime?

CAPTAIN
Murder of the duke's kinsman, Signior Mendoza.

AMBO
Nothing else? We did it, we did it, we did it!

CAPTAIN
Take heed, gentlemen, what you confess.

CLARIDIANA
I'll confess anything, since I am made a fool by a knave. I'll be hang'd like an innocent, that's flat.

ROGERO
I'll not see my shame. Hemp instead of a quacksalver. You shall put out mine eyes, and my head shall be bought to make ink-horns of.

CAPTAIN
You do confess the murder?

CLARIDIANA
Sir, 'tis true,
Done by a faithless Christian and a Jew.

CAPTAIN
To prison with them; we will hear no further;
The tongue betrays the heart of guilty murther.

[Exeunt **OMNES**.

SCENE II

Pavia.

Enter **COUNT MASSINO**, **ISABELLA**, **ANNA**, and **SERVANTS**.

MASSINO
Welcome to Pavy, sweet; and may this kiss
Chase melancholy from thy company;
Speak, my soul's joy, how fare you after travel?

ISABELLA

Like one that scapeth danger on the seas,
Yet trembles with cold fears, being safe on land,
With bare imagination of what's past.

MASSINO

Fear keep with cowards, air-stars cannot move.

ISABELLA

Fear in this kind, my lord, doth sweeten love.

MASSINO

To think fear joy, dear, I cannot conjecture.

ISABELLA

Fear's sire to fervency,
Which makes love's sweet prove nectar;
Trembling desire, fear, hope, and doubtful leisure,
Distil from love the quintessence of pleasure.

MASSINO

Madam, I yield to you; fear keeps with love,
My oratory is too weak against you:
You have the ground of knowledge, wise experience,
Which makes your argument invincible.

ISABELLA

You are Time's scholar, and can flatter weakness.

MASSINO

Custom allows it, and we plainly see
Princes and women maintain flattery.

ISABELLA

Anna, go see my jewels and my trunks
Be aptly placèd in their several rooms.

[Exit **ANNA**.

[Enter **GNIACA** Count of Gaza, with **ATTENDANTS**.

My lord,
Know you this gallant? Tis a complete gentleman.

MASSINO

I do; 'tis Count Gniaca, my endeared friend.

GNIACA

Welcome to Pavy; welcome, fairest lady.
Your sight, dear friend, is life's restorative;
This day's the period of long-wish'd content,
More welcome to me than day to the world,
Night to the wearied, or gold to a miser:
Such joy feels friendship in society.

ISABELLA [Aside]
A rare-shaped man: compare them both together.

MASSINO
Our loves are friendly twins, both at a birth;
The joy you taste, that joy do I conceive.
This day's the jubilee of my desire.

ISABELLA [Aside]
He's fairer than he was when first I saw him.
This little time makes him more excellent.

GUIDO
Relate some news. Hark you; what lady's that?
Be open-breasted, so will I to thee.

[They whisper.

ISABELLA [Aside]
Error did blind him that paints love blind;
For my love plainly judges difference:
Love is clear-sighted, and with eagle's eyes,
Undazzled, looks upon bright sun-beam'd beauty.
Nature did rob herself when she made him,
Blushing to see her work excel herself;
'Tis shape makes mankind femelacy.
Forgive me, Count Massino, 'tis my fate
To love thy friend, and quit thy love with hate.
I must enjoy him; let hope thy passions smother;
Faith cannot cool blood; I'll clip him were 't my brother.
Such is the heat of my sincere affection,
Hell nor earth can keep love in subjection!

GNIACA
I crave your honour's pardon; my ignorance
Of what you were may gain a courteous pardon.

ISABELLA
There needs no pardon where there's no offence.
[Aside]
His tongue strikes music ravishing my sense:

I must be sudden, else desire confounds me.

MASSINO
What sport affords this climate for delight?

GNIACA
We'll hawk and hunt to-day; as for to-morrow,
Variety shall feed variety.

ISABELLA
Dissimulation women's armour is,
Aid love, belief, and female constancy.—
O I am sick, my lord! Kind Massino, help me!

MASSINO
Forfend it, Heaven! Madam, sit; how fare you?
My life's best comfort, speak—O speak, sweet saint!

ISABELLA
Fetch art to keep life; run, my love, I faint;
My vital breath runs coldly through my veins;
I see lean death, with eyes imaginary,
Stand fearfully before me; here my end,
A wife unconstant, yet thy loving friend!

MASSINO
As swift as thought fly I to wish thee aid.

[Exit.

ISABELLA
Thus innocence by craft is soon betray'd.—
My Lord Gniaca, 'tis your art must heal me;
I am love-sick for your love; love, love, for loving!
I blush for speaking truth; fair sir, believe me,
Beneath the moon nought but your frown can grieve me.

GNIACA
Lady, by Heaven, methinks this fit is strange.

ISABELLA
Count not my love light for this sudden change:
By Cupid's bow I swear, and will avow,
I never knew true perfect love till now.

GNIACA
Wrong not yourself, me, and your dearest friend;
Your love is violent, and soon will end.

Love is not love unless love doth persever;
That love is perfect love that loves for ever.

ISABELLA
Such love is mine; believe it, well-shaped youth,
Though women use to lie, yet I speak truth.
Give sentence for my life, or speedy death.
Can you affect me?

GNIACA
I should belie my thoughts to give denial;
But then to friendship I must turn disloyal.
I will not wrong my friend; let that suffice.

ISABELLA
I'll be a miracle; for love a woman dies.

[Offers to stab herself.

GNIACA
Hold, madam; these are soul-killing passions.
I'd rather wrong my friend than you yourself.

ISABELLA
Love me, or else, by Jove, death's but delay'd.
My vow is fix'd in heaven; fear shall not move me;
My life is death with tortures 'less you love me.

GNIACA
Give me some respite, and I will resolve you.

ISABELLA
My heart denies it;
My blood is violent; now or else never.
Love me! and like love's queen I'll fall before thee,
Enticing dalliance from thee with my smiles,
And steal thy heart with my delicious kisses.
I'll study art in love, that in a rapture
Thy soul shall taste pleasure's excelling nature.
Love me!
Both art and nature in large recompense
Shall be profuse in ravishing thy sense.

GNIACA
You have prevail'd; I am yours from all the world;
Thy wit and beauty have entranced my soul;
I long for dalliance, my blood burns like fire.
Hell's pain on earth is to delay desire!

ISABELLA

I kiss thee for that breath. This day you hunt;
In midst of all your sports leave you Massino;
Return to me, whose life rests in thy sight,
Where pleasure shall make nectar our delight.

GNIACA

I condescend to what thy will implores me;
He that but now neglected thee adores thee.
But see, here comes my friend; fear makes him tremble.

[Enter **MASSINO**, **ANNA**, and **DOCTOR**.

ISABELLA

Women are witless that cannot dissemble:
Now I am sick again.—Where's my Lord Massino?
His love and my health's vanish'd both together.

MASSINO

Wrong not thy friend, dear friend, in thy extremes;
Here's a profound Hippocrates, my dear,
To administer to thee the spirit of health.

ISABELLA

Your sight to me, my lord, excels all physic;
I am better far, my love, than when you left me;
Your friend was comfortable to me at the last.
'Twas but a fit, my lord, and now 'tis past.
Are all things ready, sir?

ANNA

Yes, madam, the house is fit.

GNIACA

Desire in women is the life of wit.

[Exeunt **OMNES**.

SCENE III

Venice.—A Street.

Enter **ABIGAIL** and **THAIS** at several doors.

ABIGAIL

O partner, I am with child of laughter, and none but you can be my midwife. Was there ever such a game at noddy?

THAIS
Our husbands think they are foremen of the jury; they hold the heretic point of predestination, and sure they are born to be hanged!

ABIGAIL
They are like to prove men of judgment; but not for killing of him that's yet alive and well recovered.

THAIS
As soon as my man saw the watch come up,
All his spirit was down.

ABIGAIL
But though they have made us good sport in speech,
They did hinder us of good sport in action.
O wench! imagination is strong in pleasure!

THAIS
That's true; for the opinion my good man had of enjoying you made him do wonders.

ABIGAIL
Why should a weak man, that is so soon satisfied, desire variety?

THAIS
Their answer is, to feed on pheasants continually would breed a loathing.

ABIGAIL
Then if we seek for strange flesh that have stomachs at will, 'tis pardonable.

THAIS
Ay, if men had any feeling of it; but they judge us by themselves.

ABIGAIL
Well, we will bring them to the gallows, and then, like kind virgins, beg their lives; and after live at our pleasures, and this bridle shall still rein them.

THAIS
Faith, if we were disposed, we might sin as safe as if we had the broad seal to warrant it; but that night's work will stick by me this forty weeks. Come, shall we go visit the discontented Lady Lentulus, whom the Lord Mendoza has confess'd to his chirurgion he would have robb'd? I thought great men would but have robb'd the poor, yet he the rich.

ABIGAIL
He thought that the richer purchase, though with the worse conscience; but we'll to comfort her, and then go hear our husband's lamentations. They say mine has compiled an ungodly volume of satires against women, and calls his book The Snarl.

THAIS
But he's in hope his book will save him.

ABIGAIL
God defend that it should, or any that snarl in that fashion!

THAIS
Well, wench, if I could be metamorphosed into thy shape, I should have my husband pliant to me in his life, and soon rid of him; for being weary with his continual motion, he'd die of a consumption.

ABIGAIL
Make much of him, for all our wanton prize;

Follow the proverb, "Merry be and wise."

[Exeunt.

SCENE IV

Isabella's house at Pavia.

Enter **ISABELLA**, **ANNA**, and **SERVANTS**.

ISABELLA
Time, that devour'st all mortality,
Run swiftly these few hours,
And bring Gniaca on thy agèd shoulders,
That I may clip the rarest model of creation.
Do this, gentle Time,
And I will curl thine agèd silver lock,
And dally with thee in delicious pleasure:
Medea-like I will renew thy youth,
But if thy frozen steps delay my love,
I'll poison thee, with murder curse thy paths,
And make thee know a time of infamy.—
Anna, give watch, and bring me certain notice
When Count Gniaca doth approach my house.

ANNA
Madam, I go.—
I am kept for pleasure, though I never taste it;
For 'tis the usher's office still to cover
His lady's private meetings with her lover.

[Exit.

ISABELLA
Desire, thou quenchless flame that burn'st our souls,
Cease to torment me;
The dew of pleasure shall put out thy fire,
And quite consume thee with satiety.
Lust shall be cool'd with lust, wherein I'll prove
The life of love is only saved by love.

[Enter **ANNA**.

ANNA
Madam, he's coming.

ISABELLA
Thou blessed Mercury,
Prepare a banquet fit to please the gods;
Let sphere-like music breathe delicious tones
Into our mortal ears; perfume the house
With odoriferous scents, sweeter than myrrh,
Or all the spices in Panchaia.
His sight and touching we will recreate,
That his five senses shall be fivefold happy.
His breath like roses casts out sweet perfume;
Time now with pleasure shall itself consume.

[Enter **GNIACA** in his hunting weeds.

How like Adonis in his hunting weeds,
Looks this same goddess-tempter!
And art thou come? This kiss entrance thy soul!
Gods, I do not envy you; for, know this,
Way's here on earth complete, excels your bliss:
I'll not change this night's pleasure with you all.

GNIACA
Thou creature made by love, composed of pleasure,
That makest true use of thy creation,
In thee both wit and beauty's resident;
Delightful pleasure, unpeer'd excellence.
This is the fate fix'd fast unto thy birth,
That thou alone shouldst be man's heaven on earth.
If I alone may but enjoy thy love,
I'll not change earthly joy to be heaven's Jove:
For though that women-haters now are common,
They all shall know earth's joy consists in woman.

ISABELLA
My love was dotage till I lovèd thee,

For thy soul truly tastes our petulance;
Condition's lover, Cupid's Intelligencer,
That makes man understand what pleasure is:
These are fit tributes unto thy knowledge;
For women's beauty o'er men bear that rule,
Our power commands the rich, the wise, the fool.
Though scorn grows big in man, in growth and stature,
Yet women are the rarest works of nature.

GNIACA
I do confess the truth, and must admire
That women can command rare man's desire.

ISABELLA
Cease admiration, sit to Cupid's feast,
The preparation to Paphian dalliance;
Harmonious music, breathe thy silver airs
To stir up appetite to Venus' banquet,
That breath of pleasure that entrances souls,
Making that instant happiness a heaven,
In the true taste of love's deliciousness.

GNIACA
Thy words are able to stir cold desire
Into his flesh that lies entomb'd in ice,
Having lost the feeling use of warmth in blood;
Then how much more in me, whose youthful veins,
Like a proud river, overflow their bounds?
Pleasure's ambrosia, or love's nourisher,
I long for privacy; come, let us in;
'Tis custom, and not reason, makes love sin.

ISABELLA
I'll lead the way to Venus' paradise,
Where thou shalt taste that fruit that made man wise.

[Exit **ISABELLA**.

GNIACA
Sing notes of pleasure to elate our blood:
Why should heaven frown on joys that do us good?
I come, Isabella, keeper of love's treasure,
To force thy blood to lust, and ravish pleasure.

[Exit.

[After some short song, enter **ISABELLA** and **GNIACA** again, she hanging about his neck lasciviously.

GNIACA

Still I am thy captive, yet thy thoughts are free;
To be love's bondman is true liberty.
I have swum in seas of pleasure without ground,
Ventrous desire past depth itself hath drown'd.
Such skill has beauty's art in a true lover,
That dead desire to life it can recover.
Thus beauty our desire can soon advance,
Then straight again kill it with dalliance.
Divinest women, your enchanting breaths
Give lovers many lives and many deaths!

ISABELLA

May thy desire to me for ever last,
Not die but surfeit on my delicates;
And as I tie this jewel about thy neck,
So may I tie thy constant love to mine,
Never to seek weaking variety,
That greedy curse of man and woman's hell,
Where nought but shame and loath'd diseases dwell.

GNIACA

You counsel well, dear; learn it then;
For change is given more to you than men.

ISABELLA

My faith to thee, like rocks, shall never move,
The sun shall change his course ere I my love.

[Enter **ANNA**.

ANNA

Madam, the Count Massino knocks.

ISABELLA

Dear love, into my chamber, till I send
My hate from sight.

GNIACA

Lust makes me wrong my friend.

[Exit **GNIACA**.

ISABELLA

Anna, stand here and entertain Lord Massino;
I from my window straight will give him answer.
The serpent's wit to woman rest in me;
By that man fell, then why not he by me?

Feign'd sighs, and tears dropp'd from a woman's eye,
Blinds man of reason, strikes his knowledge dumb.
Wit arms a woman; Count Massino, come.

[Exit **ISABELLA**.

ANNA
My office still is under: yet in time
Ushers prove masters, degrees makes us climb.

[**MASSINO** knocks.

Who knocks? Is't you, my noble lord?

[Enter **MASSINO** in his hunting weeds.

MASSINO
Came my friend hither—Count Gniaca?

ANNA
No, my good lord.

MASSINO
Where's my Isabella?

ANNA
In her chamber.

MASSINO
Good: I'll visit her.

ANNA
The chamber's lock'd, my lord: she will be private.

MASSINO
Lock'd against me—my saucy malapert?

ANNA
Be patient, good my lord; she'll give you answer.

MASSINO
Isabella! life of love, speak, 'tis I that calls.

[**ISABELLA** at her window.

ISABELLA
I must desire your lordship pardon me.

MASSINO
Lordship? what's this? Isabella, art thou blind?

ISABELLA
My lord,
My lust was blind, but now my soul's clear-sighted,
And sees the spots that did corrupt my flesh:
Those tokens sent from hell, brought by desire,
The messenger of everlasting death!

ANNA
My lady's in her pulpit, now she'll preach.

MASSINO
Is not thy lady mad? In verity I always
Took her for a puritan, and now she shows it.

ISABELLA
Mock not repentance. Profanation
Brings mortals laughing to damnation.
Believe it, lord, Isabella's ill-pass'd life,
Like gold refined, shall make a perfect wife.
I stand on firm ground now, before on ice;
We know not virtue till we taste of vice.

MASSINO
Do you hear dissimulation, woman sinner?

ISABELLA
Leave my house, good my lord, and for my part,
I look for a most wish'd reconciliation
Betwixt myself and my most wrongèd husband.
Tempt not contrition then, religious lord.

MASSINO
Indeed I was one of your family once;
But do not I know these are but brain-tricks:
And where the devil has the fee-simple,
He'll keep possession; and will you halt
Before me that yourself has made a cripple?

ISABELLA
Nay, then, you wrong me; and, disdainèd lord,
I paid then for thy pleasures vendible—
Whose mercenary flesh I bought with coin.
I will divulge thy baseness, 'less with speed
Thou leave my house and my society.

MASSINO

Already turn'd apostate! but now all pure,
Now damn'd your faith is, and your loves endure
Like dew upon the grass; when pleasure's sun
Shines on your virtues, all your virtue's done.
I'll leave thy house and thee; go, get thee in,
Thou gaudy child of pride, and nurse of sin.

ISABELLA

Rail not on me, my lord; for if you do,
My hot desire of vengeance shall strike wonder;
Revenge in women falls like dreadful thunder!

[Exit.

ANNA

Your lordship will command me no further service?

MASSINO

I thank thee for thy watchful service past;
Thy usher-like attendance on the stairs,
Being true signs of thy humility.

ANNA

I hope I did discharge my place with care.

MASSINO

Ushers should have much wit, but little hair;
Thou hast of both sufficient: prithee leave me,
If thou hast an honest lady, commend me to her,
But she is none.

[Exit **ANNA**.

Farewell, thou private strumpet, worse than common!
Man were on earth an angel but for woman.
That sevenfold branch of hell from them doth grow;
Pride, lust, and murder, they raise from below,
With all their fellow-sins. Women are made
Of blood, without souls; when their beauties fade,
And their lust's past, avarice or bawdry
Makes them still loved; then they buy venery,
Bribing damnation, and hire brothel-slaves:
Shame's their executors, infamy their graves.
Your painting will wipe off, which art did hide,
And show your ugly shape in spite of pride.
Farewell, Isabella, poor in soul and fame,
I leave thee rich in nothing but in shame.

Then, soulless women, know, whose faiths are hollow,
Your lust being quench'd a bloody act must follow.

[Exit.

Venice.—The Senate-house.

Enter the **DUKE AMAGO**, the **CAPTAIN**, and the rest of the **WATCH**, with the **SENATORS**.

DUKE
Justice, that makes princes like the gods,
Draws us unto the senate,
That with unpartial balance we may poise
The crimes and innocence of all offenders.
Our presence can chase bribery from laws;
He best can judge that hears himself the cause.

1ST SENATOR
True, mighty duke, it best becomes our places,
To have our light from you the sun of virtue.
Subject authority, for gain, love, or fear,
Oft quits the guilty, and condemns the clear.

DUKE
The land and people's mine; the crimes being known,
I must redress; my subjects' wrong's mine own.
Call for the two suspected for the murder
Of Mendoza, our endeared kinsman,
These voluntary murderers that confess
The murder of him that is yet alive.
We'll sport with serious justice for a while;
In show we'll frown on them that make us smile.

2ND SENATOR
Bring forth the prisoners, we may hear their answers.

[Enter; brought in with **OFFICERS**, **CLARIDIANA** and **ROGERO**.

DUKE
Stand forth, you vipers, you that have suck'd blood,
And lopp'd a branch sprung from a royal tree!
What can you answer to escape tortures?

ROGERO
We have confessed the fact, my lord, to God and man,
Our ghostly father, and that worthy captain:
We beg not life, but favourable death.

DUKE
On what ground sprung your hate to him we loved?

CLARIDIANA
Upon that curse laid on Venetians, jealousy. We thought he, being a courtier, would have made us magnificoes of the right stamp, and have play'd at primero in the presence, with gold of the city brought from our Indies.

ROGERO
Nay, more, my lord, we feared that your kinsman, for a mess of sonnets, would have given the plot of us and our wives to some needy poet, and for sport and profit brought us in some Venetian comedy upon the stage.

DUKE
Our justice dwells with mercy; be not desperate.

1ST SENATOR
His highness fain would save your lives if you would see it.

ROGERO
All the law in Venice shall not save me; I will not be saved.

CLARIDIANA
Fear not, I have a trick to bring us to hanging in spite of the law.

ROGERO
Why, now I see thou lovest me; thou hast confirm'd
Thy friendship for ever to me by these words.
Why, I should never hear lanthorn and candle call'd for
But I should think it was for me and my wife.
I'll hang for that, forget not thy trick;
Upon 'em with thy trick; I long for sentence.

2ND SENATOR
Will you appeal for mercy to the duke?

CLARIDIANA
Kill not thy justice, duke, to save our lives;
We have deserved death.

ROGERO
Make not us precedents for after-wrongs;

I will receive punishment for my sins:
It shall be a means to lift me towards heaven.

CLARIDIANA
Let's have our desert; we crave no favour.

DUKE
Take them asunder; grave justice makes us mirth;
That man is soulless that ne'er smiles on earth.
Signor Rogero, relate the weapon you kill'd him with, and the manner.

ROGERO
My lord, your lustful kinsman—I can title him no better—came sneaking to my house like a promoter to spy flesh in the Lent. Now I, having a Venetian spirit, watch'd my time, and with my rapier run him through, knowing all pains are but trifles to the horn of a citizen.

DUKE
Take him aside. Signior Claridiana, what weapon had you for this bloody act? What dart used death?

CLARIDIANA
My lord, I brain'd him with a cleaver my neighbour lent me, and he stood by and cried, "Strike home, old boy."

DUKE
With several instruments. Bring them face to face.
With what kill'd you our nephew?

ROGERO
With a rapier, liege.

CLARIDIANA
'Tis a lie;
I kill'd him with a cleaver, and thou stood'st by.

ROGERO
Dost think to save me and hang thyself? No, I scorn it; is this the trick thou said'st thou had'st? I kill'd him, duke. He only gave consent: 'twas I that did it.

CLARIDIANA
Thou hast always been cross to me, and wilt be to my death. Have I taken all this pains to bring thee to hanging, and dost thou slip now?

ROGERO
We shall never agree in a tale till we come to the gallows, then we shall jump.

CLARIDIANA
I'll show you a cross-point, if you cross me thus, when thou shalt not see it.

ROGERO
I'll make a wry mouth at that, or it shall cost me a fall. 'Tis thy pride to be hang'd alone, because thou scorn'st my company; but it shall be known I am as good a man as thyself, and in these actions will keep company with thy betters, Jew.

CLARIDIANA
Monster!

ROGERO
Dog-killer!

CLARIDIANA
Fencer!

[They bustle.

DUKE
Part them, part 'em!

ROGERO
Hang us, and quarter us; we shall ne'er be parted till then.

DUKE
You do confess the murder done by both?

CLARIDIANA [Aside]
But that I would not have the slave laugh at me,
And count me a coward, I have a good mind to live.
But I am resolute: 'tis but a turn.—
I do confess.

ROGERO
So do I.
Pronounce our doom, we are prepared to die.

1ST SENATOR
We sentence you to hang till you be dead;
Since you were men eminent in place and worth,
We give a Christian burial to you both.

CLARIDIANA
Not in one grave together, we beseech you, we shall ne'er agree.

ROGERO
He scorns my company till the day of judgment; I'll not hang with him.

DUKE
You hang together, that shall make you friends;

An everlasting hatred death soon ends.
To prison with them till the death;
Kings' words, like fate, must never change their breath.

ROGERO
You malice-monger, I'll be hang'd afore thee,
And 't be but to vex thee.

CLARIDIANA
I'll do you as good a turn, or the hangman and I shall fall out.

[Exeunt **AMBO**, guarded.

DUKE
Now to our kinsman, shame to royal blood;
Bring him before us.

[Enter **MENDOZA** in his nightgown and cap, guarded, with the **CAPTAIN**.

Theft in a prince is sacrilege to honour;
'Tis virtue's scandal, death of royalty.
I blush to see my shame. Nephew, sit down.
Justice, that smiles on those, on him must frown!
Speak freely, captain; where found you him wounded?

CAPTAIN
Between the widow's house and these cross neighbours;
Besides, an artificial ladder made of ropes
Was fasten'd to her window, which he confess'd
He brought to rob her of jewels and coin.
My knowledge yields no further circumstance.

DUKE
Thou know'st too much; would I were past all knowledge,
I might forget my grief springs from my shame!
Thou monster of my blood, answer in brief
To these assertions made against thy life.
Is thy soul guilty of so base a fact?

MENDOZA
I do confess I did intend to rob her;
In the attempt I fell and hurt myself.
Law's thunder is but death; I dread it not,
So my Lentulus' honour be preserved
From black suspicion of a lustful night.

DUKE
Thy head's thy forfeit for thy heart's offence;

Thy blood's prerogative may claim that favour.
Thy person then to death doom'd by just laws;
Thy death is infamous, but worse the cause.

[Exeunt.

SCENE II

Pavia.—Isabella's house.

Enter **ISABELLA** alone, **GNIACA** following her.

ISABELLA
O Heavens, that I was born to be hate's slave,
The food of rumour that devours my fame!
I am call'd Insatiate Countess, lust's paramour,
A glorious devil, and the noble whore!
I am sick, vex'd, and tormented. O revenge!

GNIACA
On whom would my Isabella be revenged?

ISABELLA
Upon a viper, that does eat mine honour;
I will not name him till I be revenged.
See, here's the libels are divulg'd against me—
An everlasting scandal to my name—
And thus the villain writes in my disgrace:—

[She reads.

Who loves Isabella the Insatiate,
Needs Atlas' back for to content her lust,
That wand'ring strumpet, and chaste wedlock's hate,
That renders truth deceit for loyal trust;
That sacrilegious thief to Hymen's rites,
Making her lust her god, heaven her delights!
Swell not, proud heart, I'll quench thy grief in blood;
Desire in woman cannot be withstood.

GNIACA
I'll be thy champion, sweet, 'gainst all the world;
Name but the villain that defames thee thus.

ISABELLA
Dare thy hand execute whom my tongue condemns,

Then art thou truly valiant, mine for ever;
But if thou faint'st, hate must our true lover sever.

GNIACA
By my dead father's soul, my mother's virtues,
And by my knighthood and gentility,
I'll be revenged
On all the authors of your obloquy!
Name him.

ISABELLA
Massino.

GNIACA
Ha!

ISABELLA
What! does his name affright thee, coward lord!
Be mad, Isabella! curse on thy revenge!
This lord was knighted for his father's worth,
Not for his own.
Farewell, thou perjured man! I'll leave you all;
You all conspire to work mine honour's fall.

GNIACA
Stay, my Isabella; were he my father's son,
Composed of me, he dies!
Delight still keep with thee. Go in.

ISABELLA
Thou art just;
Revenge to me is sweeter now than lust.

[Exit **ISABELLA**.

[Enter **MASSINO**; they see one another and draw and make a pass; then enter **ANNA**.

ANNA
What mean you, nobles? Will you kill each other?

AMBO
Hold!

MASSINO
Thou shame to friendship, what intends thy hate?

GNIACA
Love arms my hand, makes my soul valiant!

Isabella's wrongs now sit upon my sword,
To fall more heavy to thy coward's head
Than thunderbolts upon Jove's rifted oaks.
Deny thy scandal, or defend thy life.

MASSINO
What?—hath thy faith and reason left thee both,
That thou art only flesh without a soul?
Hast thou no feeling of thyself and me?
Blind rage, that will not let thee see thyself!

GNIACA
I come not to dispute but execute:
And thus comes death!

[Another pass.

MASSINO
And thus I break thy dart.
Here's at thy whore's face!

GNIACA
'Tis miss'd. Here's at thy heart!
Stay, let us breathe.

MASSINO
Let reason govern rage yet, let us leave;
Although most wrong be mine, I can forgive.
In this attempt thy shame will ever live.

GNIACA
Thou hast wrong'd the Phœnix of all women rarest—
She that's most wise, most loving, chaste, and fairest.

MASSINO
Thou dotest upon a devil, not a woman,
That has bewitch'd thee with her sorcery,
And drown'd thy soul in lethy faculties.
Her quenchless lust has quite benumbed thy knowledge;
Thy intellectual powers oblivion smothers,
That thou art nothing but forgetfulness.

GNIACA
What's this to my Isabella? My sin's mine own.
Her faults were none, until thou madest 'em known.

MASSINO
Leave her, and leave thy shame where first thou found'st it;

Else live a bondslave to diseasèd lust,
Devour'd in her gulf-like appetite,
And infamy shall write thy epitaph;
Thy memory leave nothing but thy crimes—
A scandal to thy name in future times.

GNIACA
Put up your weapon; I dare hear you further.
Insatiate lust is sire still to murther.

MASSINO
Believe it, friend, if her heart-blood were vext,
Though you kill me, new pleasure makes you next.
She loved me dearer than she loves you now;
She'll ne'er be faithful, has twice broke her vow.
This curse pursues female adultery,
They'll swim through blood for sin's variety;
Their pleasure like a sea, groundless and wide,
A woman's lust was never satisfied.

GNIACA
Fear whispers in my breast, I have a soul
That blushes red for tend'ring bloody facts.
Forgive me, friend, if I can be forgiven;
Thy counsel is the path leads me to heaven.

MASSINO
I do embrace thy reconcilèd love——

GNIACA
That death or danger now shall ne'er remove.
Go tell thy Insatiate Countess, Anna,
We have escap'd the snares of her false love,
Vowing for ever to abandon her.

MASSINO
You have heard our resolution; pray, be gone.

ANNA
My office ever rested at your pleasure;
I was the Indian, yet you had the treasure.
My faction often sweats, and oft takes cold;
Then gild true diligence o'er with gold.

MASSINO
Thy speech deserves it. There's gold;

[Gives her gold.

Be honest now, and not love's noddy,
Turn'd up and play'd on whilst thou keep'st the stock.
Prithee formally let's ha' thy absence.

ANNA
Lords, farewell.

[Exit **ANNA**.

MASSINO
'Tis whores and panders that makes earth like hell.

GNIACA
Now I am got out of lust's labyrinth,
I will to Venice for a certain time,
To recreate my much abusèd spirits,
And then revisit Pavy and my friend.

MASSINO
I'll bring you on your way, but must return;
Love is like Ætna, and will ever burn.
Yet now desire is quench'd, flamed once in height:
Till man knows hell he never has firm faith.

[Exeunt **AMBO**.

SCENE III

The balcony of Isabella's house at Pavia.

Enter **ISABELLA** raving, and **ANNA**.

ISABELLA
Out, screech-owl, messenger of my revenge's death!
Thou dost belie Gniaca; 'tis not so.

ANNA
Upon mine honesty, they are united.

ISABELLA
Thy honesty?—thou vassal to my pleasure,
Take that!

[Strikes her.

Darest thou control me when I say no?
Art not my footstool—did not I create thee,
And made thee gentle, being born a beggar?
Thou hast been my woman's pander for a crown,
And dost thou stand upon thy honesty?

ANNA
I am what you please, madam; yet 'tis so.

ISABELLA
Slave, I will slit thy tongue, 'less thou say no!

ANNA
No, no, no, madam.

ISABELLA
I have my humour, though thy no be false.
Faint-hearted coward, get thee from my sight!
When, villain? Haste, and come not near me.

ANNA
Madam, I run;—her sight like death doth fear me.

[Exit.

ISABELLA
Perfidious cowards, stain of nobility!
Venetians, and be reconciled with words!
O that I had Gniaca once more here,
Within this prison made of flesh and bone,
I'd not trust thunder with my fell revenge,
But mine own hands should do the dire exploit,
And fame should chronicle a woman's acts!
My rage respects the persons, not the facts:
Their place and worths hath power to defame me;
Mean hate is stingless, and does only name me:
I not regard it. 'Tis high blood that swells,
Give me revenge, and damn me into hells!

[Enter **DON SAGO**, a Coronel, with a band of **SOLDIERS** and a **LIEUTENANT**.

A gallant Spaniard, I will hear him speak;
Grief must be speechless, ere the heart can break!

DON SAGO
Lieutenant, let good discipline be used
In quart'ring of our troops within the city—
Not separated into many streets.

That shows weak love, but not sound policy:
Division in small numbers makes all weak;
Forces united are the nerves of war.
Mother and nurse of observation—
Whose rare ingenious sprite fills all the world,
By looking on itself with piercing eyes—
Will look through strangers' imbecilities.
Therefore be careful.

LIEUTENANT
All shall be order'd fitting your command,
For these three gifts which makes a soldier rare,
Is love and duty with a valiant care.

[Exeunt **LIEUTENANT** and **SOLDIERS**.

DON SAGO
What rarity of women feeds my sight,
And leads my senses in a maze of wonder?

[Sees **ISABELLA**.

Bellona,
Thou wert my mistress till I saw that shape;
But now my sword I'll consecrate to her,
Leave Mars and become Cupid's martialist.
Beauty can turn the rugged face of War,
And make him smile upon delightful Peace,
Courting her smoothly like a femalist.
I grow a slave unto my potent love,
Whose power change hearts, make our fate remove.

ISABELLA
Revenge, not pleasure, now o'er-rules my blood;
Rage shall drown faint love in a crimson flood;
And were he caught, I'd make him murder's hand!

DON SAGO
Methinks 'twere joy to die at her command.
I'll speak to hear her speech, whose powerful breath
Is able to infuse life into death.

ISABELLA
He comes to speak: he's mine; by love he is mine!

DON SAGO
Lady, think bold intrusion courtesy;
'Tis but imagination alters them;

Then 'tis your thoughts, not I, that do offend.

ISABELLA
Sir, your intrusion yet 's but courtesy,
Unless your future humour alter it.

DON SAGO
Why then, divinest woman, know my soul
Is dedicated to thy shrine of beauty,
To pray for mercy, and repent the wrongs
Done against love and female purity.
Thou abstract, drawn from nature's empty storehouse,
I am thy slave; command my sword, my heart;
The soul is tried best by the body's smart.

ISABELLA
You are a stranger to this land and me.
What madness is't for me to trust you then?
To cozen women is a trade 'mongst men;
Smooth promises, faint passions, with a lie,
Deceives our sex of fame and chastity.
What danger durst you hazard for my love?

DON SAGO
Perils that ever mortal durst approve.
I'll double all the works of Hercules,
Expose myself in combat against an host,
Meet danger in a place of certain death,
Yet never shrink, or give way to my fate;
Bare-breasted meet the murderous Tartar's dart,
Or any fatal engine made for death:
Such power has love and beauty from your eye,
He that dies resolute does never die!
'Tis fear gives death his strength, which I resisted,
Death is but empty air the fates have twisted.

ISABELLA
Dare you revenge my quarrel 'gainst a foe?

DON SAGO
Then ask me if I dare embrace you thus,
Or kiss your hand, or gaze on your bright eye,
Where Cupid dances on those globes of love!
Fear is my vassal; when I frown he flies;
A hundred times in life a coward dies!

ISABELLA
I not suspect your valour, but your will.

DON SAGO
To gain your love my father's blood I'll spill.

ISABELLA
Many have sworn the like, yet broke their vow.

DON SAGO
My whole endeavour to your wish shall bow;
I am your plague to scourge your enemies.

ISABELLA
Perform your promise, and enjoy your pleasure;
Spend my love's dowry, that is women's treasure;
But if thy resolution dread the trial,
I'll tell the world a Spaniard was disloyal.

DON SAGO
Relate your grief; I long to hear their names
Whose bastard spirits thy true worth defames.
I'll wash thy scandal off when their hearts bleeds;
Valour makes difference betwixt words and deeds.
Tell thy fame's poison, blood shall wash thee white.

ISABELLA
My spotless honour is a slave to spite.
These are the monsters Venice doth bring forth,
Whose empty souls are bankrupt of true worth:
False Count Guido, treacherous Gniaca,
Counties of Gazia, and of rich Massino.
Then, if thou beest a knight, help the oppress'd;
Through danger safety comes, through trouble rest.
And so my love—

DON SAGO
Ignoble villains! their best blood shall prove,
Revenge falls heavy that is raised by love!

ISABELLA
Think what reproach is to a woman's name,
Honour'd by birth, by marriage, and by beauty;
Be god on earth, and revenge innocence.
O, worthy Spaniard, on my knees I beg,
Forget the persons, think on their offence!

DON SAGO
By the white soul of honour, by heav'n's Jove,
They die if their death can attain your love!

ISABELLA

Thus will I clip thy waist—embrace thee thus;
Thus dally with thy hair, and kiss thee thus:
Our pleasures, Protean-like, in sundry shapes
Shall with variety stir dalliance.

DON SAGO

I am immortal. O, divinest creature,
Thou dost excel the gods in wit and feature!
False counts, you die, revenge now shakes his rods;
Beauty condemns you—stronger than the gods.

ISABELLA

Come, Mars of lovers, Vulcan is not here;
Make vengeance, like my bed, quite void of fear.

DON SAGO

My senses are entranced, and in this slumber
I taste heav'n's joys, but cannot count the number.

[Exeunt **AMBO**.

SCENE IV

Venice.—A street.

Enter **LADY LENTULUS**, **ABIGAIL**, and **THAIS**.

ABIGAIL

Well, madam, you see the destiny that follows marriage:
Our husbands are quiet now, and must suffer the law.

THAIS

If my husband had been worth the begging, some courtier would have had him; he might be begg'd well
enough, for he knows not his own wife from another.

LADY LENTULUS

O, you're a couple of trusty wenches, to deceive your husbands thus!

ABIGAIL

If we had not deceived them thus, we had been truss'd wenches.

THAIS

Our husbands will be hang'd, because they think themselves cuckolds.

ABIGAIL
If all true cuckolds were of that mind, the hangman would be the richest occupation, and more wealthy widows than there be younger brothers to marry them.

THAIS
The merchant venturers would be a very small company.

ABIGAIL
'Tis twelve to one of that; however the rest 'scape, I shall fear a massacre.

THAIS
If my husband hereafter, for his wealth, chance to be dubb'd, I'll have him call'd the knight of the supposed horn.

ABIGAIL
Faith, and it sounds well.

LADY LENTULUS
Come, madcaps, leave jesting, and let's deliver them out of their earthly purgation; you are the spirits that torment them; but my love and lord, kind Mendoza, will lose his life to preserve mine honour, not for hate to others.

ABIGAIL
By my troth, if I had been his judge, I should have hang'd him, for having no more wit; I speak as I think, for I would not be hang'd for ne'er a man under the heav'ns.

THAIS
Faith, I think I should for my husband: I do not hold the opinion of the philosopher, that writes, we love them best that we enjoy first; for I protest I love my husband better than any that did know me before.

ABIGAIL
So do I; yet life and pleasure are two sweet things to a woman.

LADY LENTULUS
He that's willing to die to save mine honour, I'll die to save his.

ABIGAIL
Tut, believe it who that list, we love a lively man, I grant you; but to maintain that life I'll ne'er consent to die.
This is a rule I still will keep in breast,
Love well thy husband, wench, but thyself best!

THAIS
I have followed your counsel hitherto, and mean to do still.

LADY LENTULUS
Come, we neglect our business; 'tis no jesting;
To-morrow they are executed 'less we reprieve them.

We be their destinies to cast their fate.
Let's all go.

ABIGAIL
I fear not to come late.

[Exeunt.

SCENE V

Pavia.—A street.

Enter **DON SAGO** solus, with a case of pistols.

DON SAGO
Day was my night, and night must be my day;
The sun shined on my pleasure with my love,
And darkness must lend aid to my revenge.
The stage of heaven is hung with solemn black,
A time best fitting to act tragedies.
The night's great queen, that maiden governess,
Musters black clouds to hide her from the world,
Afraid to look on my bold enterprise.
Cursed creatures, messengers of death, possess the world;
Night-ravens, screetch-owls, and voice-killing mandrakes,
The ghosts of misers, that imprison'd gold
Within the harmless bowels of the earth,
Are night's companions. Bawds to lust and murder,
Be all propitious to my act of justice
Upon the scandalisers of her fame,
That is the lifeblood of deliciousness,
Deem'd Isabella, Cupid's treasurer,
Whose soul contains the richest gifts of love:
Her beauty from my heart fear doth expel:
They relish pleasure best that dread not hell!
Who's there?

[Enter **COUNT MASSINO**.

MASSINO
A friend to thee, if thy intents
Be just and honourable.

DON SAGO
Count Massino, speak, I am the watch.

MASSINO

My name is Massino: dost thou know me?

DON SAGO

Yes, slanderous villain, nurse of obloquy,
Whose poison'd breath has speckled clear-faced virtue,
And made a leper of Isabella's fame,
That is as spotless as the eye of heaven!
Thy vital thread's a-cutting; start not, slave;
He's sure of sudden death, Heaven cannot save!

MASSINO

Art not Gniaca turn'd apostata?
Has pleasure once again turned thee again
A devil? art not Gniaca—hah?

DON SAGO

O that I were, then would I stab myself,
For he is mark'd for death as well as thee!
I am Don Sago, thy mortal enemy,
Whose hand love makes thy executioner!

MASSINO

I know thee, valiant Spaniard, and to thee
Murder's more hateful than is sacrilege.
Thy actions ever have been honourable.

DON SAGO

And this the crown of all my actions,
To purge the earth of such a man turn'd monster!

MASSINO

I never wrong'd thee, Spaniard—did I? speak:
Tell him all the plot.
I'll make thee satisfaction like a soldier,
A true Italian, and a gentleman.
Thy rage is treachery without a cause.

DON SAGO

My rage is just, and thy heart blood shall know,
He that wrongs beauty, must be honour's foe.
Isabel's quarrel arms the Spaniard's spirit!

MASSINO

Murder should keep with baseness, not with merit.
I'll answer thee to-morrow, by my soul,
And clear thy doubts, or satisfy thy will.

DON SAGO
He's war's best scholar can with safety kill.
Take this to-night; now meet with me to-morrow.

[Shoots. **MASSINO** falls dead.

I come, Isabella; half thy hate is dead;
Valour makes murder light, which fear makes lead.

[Enter **CAPTAIN** with a band of **SOLDIERS**.

CAPTAIN
The pistol was shot here; seize him!
Bring lights. What, Don Sago, colonel of the horse?
Ring the alarum-bell, raise the whole city;
His troops are in the town; I fear treachery.
Who's this lies murder'd? Speak, bloodthirsty Spaniard!

DON SAGO
I have not spoil'd his face, you may know his visnomy.

CAPTAIN
'Tis Count Massino; go convey him hence;
Thy life, proud Spaniard, answers this offence.
A strong guard for the prisoner, 'less the city's powers
Rise to rescue him!

[Begirt him with **SOLDIERS**.

DON SAGO
What needs this strife?
Know, slaves, I prize revenge above my life.
Fame's register to future times shall tell
That by Don Sago, Count Massino fell!

[Exeunt **OMNES**.

Pavia.—The place of execution.

Enter **MEDINA**, followed by soldiers with the dead body of **COUNT MASSINO** on a bier; **DON SAGO** guarded, **EXECUTIONER**. A scaffold laid out.

MEDINA

Don Sago, quakest thou not to behold this spectacle—
This innocent sacrifice, murder'd nobleness—
When blood, the Maker ever promiseth,
Shall though with slow yet with sure vengeance rest?
'Tis a guerdon earn'd, and must be paid;
As sure revenge, as it is sure a deed;
I ne'er knew murder yet, but it did bleed.
Canst thou, after so many fearful conflicts
Between this object and thy guilty conscience,
Now thou art freed from out the serpent's jaws,
That vild adulteress, whose sorceries
Doth draw chaste men into incontinence—
Whose tongue flows over with harmful eloquence—
Canst thou, I say, repent this heinous act,
And learn to loathe that killing cockatrice?

DON SAGO

By this fresh blood, that from thy manly breast
I cowardly sluiced out, I would in hell,
From this sad minute till the day of doom,
To re-inspire vain Æsculapius,
And fill these crimson conduits, feel the fire
Due to the damnèd and this horrid fact!

MEDINA

Upon my soul, brave Spaniard, I believe thee.

DON SAGO

O cease to weep in blood, or teach me too!
The bubbling wounds do murmur for revenge.
This is the end of lust, where men may see,
Murder's the shadow of adultery,
And follows it to death.

MEDINA

But, hopeful lord, we do commiserate
Thy bewitch'd fortunes, a free pardon give
On this thy true and noble penitence.
Withal we make thee colonel of our horse,
Levied against the proud Venetian state.

DON SAGO

Medina, I thank thee not; give life to him
That sits with Risus and the full-cheek'd Bacchus,
The rich and mighty monarchs of the earth;
To me life is ten times more terrible
Than death can be to me. O, break, my breast!

Divines and dying men may talk of hell,
But in my heart the several torments dwell.
What Tanais, Nilus, or what Tigris swift,
What Rhenus ferier than the cataract,—
Although Neptolis cold, the waves of all the Northern Sea,
Should flow for ever through these guilty hands,
Yet the sanguinolent stain would extant be!

MEDINA
God pardon thee! we do.

[Enter a **MESSENGER**.

MESSENGER
The countess comes, my lord, unto the death;

[A shout.

But so unwillingly and unprepared,
That she is rather forced, thinking the sum
She sent to you of twenty thousand pound
Would have assurèd her of life.

MEDINA
O Heavens!
Is she not weary yet of lust and life?
Had it been Crœsus' wealth, she should have died;
Her goods by law are all confiscate to us,
And die she shall: her lust
Would make a slaughter-house of Italy.
Ere she attain'd to four-and-twenty years,
Three earls, one viscount, and this valiant Spaniard,
Are known to ha' been the fuel to her lust;
Besides her secret lovers, which charitably
I judge to have been but few, but some they were.
Here is a glass wherein to view her soul,
A noble but unfortunate gentleman,
Cropp'd by her hand, as some rude passenger
Doth pluck the tender roses in the bud!
Murder and lust, the least of which is death,
And hath she yet any false hope of breath?

[Enter **ISABELLA**, with her hair hanging down, a chaplet of flowers on her head, a nosegay in her hand;
EXECUTIONER before her, and with her a **CARDINAL**.

ISABELLA
What place is this?

CARDINAL
Madam, the Castle Green.

ISABELLA
There should be dancing on a green, I think.

CARDINAL
Madam,
To you none other than your dance of death.

ISABELLA
Good my Lord Cardinal, do not thunder thus;
I sent to-day to my physician,
And, as he says, he finds no sign of death.

CARDINAL
Good madam, do not jest away your soul.

ISABELLA
O servant, how hast thou betray'd my life!
[To **SAGO**]
Thou art my dearest lover now, I see;
Thou wilt not leave me till my very death.
Bless'd be thy hand! I sacrifice a kiss
To it and vengeance. Worthily thou didst;
He died deservedly. Not content to enjoy
My youth and beauty, riches and my fortune,
But like a chronicler of his own vice,
In epigrams and songs he tuned my name,
Renown'd me for a strumpet in the courts
Of the French King and the great Emperor.
Did'st thou not kill him drunk?

MEDINA
O shameless woman!

ISABELLA
Thou should'st, or in the embraces of his lust;
It might have been a woman's vengeance.
Yet I thank thee, Sago, and would not wish him living
Were my life instant ransom.

CARDINAL
Madam, in your soul
Have charity.

ISABELLA
There's money for the poor.

[Gives him money.

CARDINAL
O lady, this is but a branch of charity,
An ostentation, or a liberal pride:
Let me instruct your soul, for that, I fear,
Within the painted sepulchre of flesh,
Lies in a dead consumption. Good madam, read.

[Gives a book.

ISABELLA
You put me to my book, my lord; will not that save me?

CARDINAL
Yes, madam, in the everlasting world.

DON SAGO
Amen, amen!

ISABELLA
While thou wert my servant, thou hast ever said
Amen to all my wishes. Witness this spectacle.
Where's my lord Medina?

MEDINA
Here, Isabella. What would you?

ISABELLA
May we not be reprieved?

MEDINA
Mine honour's past; you may not.

ISABELLA
No, 'tis my honour past.

MEDINA
Thine honour's past, indeed.

ISABELLA
Then there's no hope of absolute remission?

MEDINA
For that your holy confessor will tell you;
Be dead to this world, for I swear you die,
Were you my father's daughter.

ISABELLA

Can you do nothing, my Lord Cardinal?

CARDINAL

More than the world, sweet lady; help to save
What hand of man wants power to destroy.

ISABELLA

You're all for this world, then why not I?
Were you in health and youth, like me, my lord,
Although you merited the crown of life,
And stood in state of grace assured of it,
Yet in this fearful separation,
Old as you are, e'en till your latest gasp,
You'd crave the help of the physician,
And wish your days lengthen'd one summer longer.
Though all be grief, labour, and misery,
Yet none will part with it, that I can see.

MEDINA

Up to the scaffold with her, 'tis late.

ISABELLA

Better late than never, my good lord; you think
You use square dealing, Medina's mighty duke,
Tyrant of France, sent hither by the devil.

[She ascends the scaffold.

MEDINA

The fitter to meet you.

CARDINAL

Peace! Good my lord, in death do not provoke her.

ISABELLA

Servant,
Low as my destiny I kneel to thee,
[To **SAGO**]
Honouring in death thy manly loyalty;
And what so e'er become of my poor soul,
The joys of both worlds evermore be thine.
Commend me to the noble Count Gniaca,
That should have shared thy valour and my hatred:
Tell him I pray his pardon, and—
Medina, art thou yet inspired from heaven?
Show thy Creator's image: be like Him,

Father of mercy.

MEDINA
Head's-man, do thine office.

ISABELLA
Now God lay all thy sins upon thy head,
And sink thee with them to infernal darkness,
Thou teacher of the furies' cruelty!

CARDINAL
O madam, teach yourself a better prayer;
This is your latest hour.

ISABELLA
He is mine enemy, his sight torments me;
I shall not die in quiet.

MEDINA
I'll be gone: off with her head there!

[Exit.

ISABELLA
Takest thou delight to torture misery?
Such mercy find thou in the day of doom.

SAGO
My lord, here is a holy friar desires
To have some conference with the prisoners.

[Enter **ROBERTO**, Count of Cyprus, in friar's weeds.

ROBERTO
It is in private, what I have to say,
With favour of your fatherhood.

CARDINAL
Friar, in God's name, welcome.

[**ROBERTO** ascends to **ISABELLA**.

ROBERTO
Lady, it seems your eye is still the same—
Forgetful of what most it should behold.
Do not you know me, then?

ISABELLA

Holy sir,
So far you are gone from my memory,
I must take truce with time ere I can know you.

ROBERTO
Bear record, all you blessèd saints in heaven,
I come not to torment thee in thy death;
For of himself he's terrible enough.
But call to mind a lady like yourself;
And think how ill in such a beauteous soul,
Upon the instant morrow of her nuptials,
Apostasy and vild revolt would show:
Withal imagine that she had a lord,
Jealous the air should ravish her chaste looks:
Doting like the creator in his models,
Who views them every minute, and with care
Mix'd in his fear of their obedience to him.
Suppose her sung through famous Italy,
More common than the looser songs of Petrarch,
To every several zany's instrument;
And he, poor wretch, hoping some better fate
Might call her back from her adulterate purpose,
Lives in obscure and almost unknown life,
Till hearing that she is condemn'd to die—
For he once loved her—lends his pinèd corpse
Motion to bring him to her stage of honour,
Where drown'd in woe at her so dismal chance,
He clasps her: thus he falls into a trance.

ISABELLA
O, my offended lord, lift up your eyes:
But yet avert them from my loathèd sight.
Had I with you enjoyed the lawful pleasure,
To which belongs nor fear nor public shame,
I might have lived in honour, died in fame!
Your pardon on my falt'ring knees I beg,
Which shall confirm more peace unto my death
Than all the grave instructions of the Church.

ROBERTO
Pardon belongs unto my holy weeds,
Freely thou hast it.
Farewell, my Isabella! let thy death
Ransom thy soul. O die a rare example!
The kiss thou gavest me in the church, here take;
As I leave thee, so thou the world forsake!

[Exit **ROBERTO**.

CARDINAL

Rare accident, ill welcome, noble lord.
Madam, your executioner desires you to forgive him.

ISABELLA

Yes, and give him too. What must I do, my friend?

EXECUTIONER

Madam, only tie up your hair.

ISABELLA

O, these golden nets,
That have ensnared so many wanton youths,
Not one but has been held a thread of life,
And superstitiously depended on.
Now to the block we must vail! What else?

EXECUTIONER

Madam, I must entreat you, blind your eyes.

ISABELLA

I have lived too long in darkness, my friend;
And yet mine eyes, with their majestic light,
Have got new muses in a poet's sprite.
They have been more gazed at than the god of day:
Their brightness never could be flatterèd,
Yet thou command'st a fixèd cloud of lawn
To eclipse eternally these minutes of light.
What else?

EXECUTIONER

Now, madam, all's done,
And when you please, I'll execute my office.

ISABELLA

We will be for thee straight.
Give me your blessing, my Lord Cardinal.
Lord, I am well prepared:
Murder and lust, down with my ashes sink,
But, like ingrateful seed, perish in earth,
That you may never spring against my soul,
Like weeds to choke it in the heavenly harvest.
I fall to rise; mount to thy Maker, spirit!
Leave here thy body, death has her demerit.

[The **EXECUTIONER** strikes off her head.

CARDINAL
A host of angels be thy convey hence.

[Re-enter **MEDINA**.

MEDINA
To funeral with her body and this lord's.
None here, I hope, can tax us of injustice:
She died deservedly, and may like fate
Attend all women so insatiate.

[Exeunt **OMNES**.

SCENE II

Venice.—The Senate-house.

Enter **AMAGO THE DUKE**, the **WATCH**, and **SENATORS**.

DUKE
I am amazèd at this maze of wonder,
Wherein no thread or clue presents itself,
To wind us from the obscure passages.
What says my nephew?

WATCH
Still resolute, my lord, and doth confess the theft.

DUKE
We'll use him like a felon; cut him off,
For fear he do pollute our sounder parts.
Yet why should he steal,
That is a loaden vine? Riches to him
Were adding sands into the Libyan shore,
Or far less charity. What say the other prisoners?

WATCH
Like men, my lord, fit for the other world,
They take't upon their death, they slew your nephew.

DUKE
And he is yet alive; keep them asunder;
We may scent out the wile.

[Enter **CLARIDIANA** and **ROGERO** bound; with a **FRIAR** and **OFFICERS**.

ROGERO
My friend, is it the rigour of the law
I should be tied thus hard, I'll undergo it;
If not, prithee then slacken. Yet I have deserved it;
This murder lies heavy on my conscience.

CLARIDIANA
Wedlock, ay, here's my wedlock! O whore, whore, whore!

FRIAR
O, sir, be qualified.

CLARIDIANA
Sir, I am to die a dog's death, and will snarl a little at the old signor. You are only a parenthesis, which I will leave out of my execrations; but first to our quondam wives, that makes us cry our vowels in red capital letters, "I and U are cuckolds!" O may bastard-bearing, with the pangs of childbirth, be doubled to 'em! May they have ever twins, and be three week in travail between! May they be so rivell'd with painting by that time they are thirty, that it may be held a work of condign merit but to look upon 'em! May they live to ride in triumph in a dung-cart, and be brown'd with all the odious ceremonies belonging to 't! may the cucking-stool be their recreation, and a dungeon their dying-chamber! May they have nine lives like a cat, to endure this and more! May they be burnt for witches of a sudden! And lastly, may the opinion of philosophers prove true, that women have no souls!

[Enter **THAIS** and **ABIGAIL**.

THAIS
What, husband—at your prayers so seriously?

CLARIDIANA
Yes, a few orisons. Friar, thou that stand'st between the soul of men and the devil, keep these female spirits away, or I will renounce my faith else.

ABIGAIL
O husband, I little thought to see you in this taking!

ROGERO
O whore, I little thought to see you in this taking! I am governor of this castle of cornets; my grave will be stumbled at, thou adult'rate whore! I might have lived like a merchant.

ABIGAIL
So you may still, husband.

ROGERO
Peace! thou art very quick with me.

ABIGAIL
Ay, by my faith, and so I am, husband; belike you know I am with child.

ROGERO

A bastard, a bastard, a bastard! I might have lived like a gentleman, and now I must die like a hanger on, show tricks upon a wooden horse, and run through an alphabet of scurvy faces! Do not expect a good look from me.

ABIGAIL

O me unfortunate!

CLARIDIANA

O to think, whilst we are singing the last hymn, and ready to be turn'd off, some new tune is inventing by some metremonger, to a scurvy ballad of our death! Again, at our funeral sermons, to have the divine divide his text into fair branches! O, flesh and blood cannot endure it! Yet I will take it patiently like a grave man. Hangman, tie not my halter of a true lover's knot: I burst it if thou dost.

THAIS

Husband, I do beseech you on my knees,
I may but speak with you. I'll win your pardon,
Or with tears, like Niobe, bedew a—

CLARIDIANA

Hold thy water, crocodile, and say I am bound to do thee no harm; were I free, yet I could not be looser than thou; for thou art a whore! Agamemnon's daughter, that was sacrificed for a good wind, felt but a blast of the torments thou should'st endure; I'd make thee swound oftener than that fellow that by his continual practice hopes to become drum-major. What sayst thou to tickling to death with bodkins? But thou hast laugh'd too much at me already, whore! Justice, O duke! and let me not hang in suspense.

ABIGAIL

Husband,
I'll nail me to the earth, but I'll win your pardon.
My jewels, jointure, all I have shall fly;
Apparel, bedding, I'll not leave a rug,
So you may come off fairly.

CLARIDIANA

I'll come off fairly: thou beg my pardon! I had rather Chirurgeons' Hall should beg my dead body for an anatomy than thou beg my life. Justice, O duke! and let us die!

DUKE

Signior, think, and dally not with heaven,
But freely tell us, did you do the murder?

ROGERO

I have confess'd it to my ghostly father,
And done the sacrament of penance for it.
What would your highness more?

CLARIDIANA

The like have I; what would your highness more?

And here before you all take't o' my death.

DUKE
In God's name, then, on to the death with them.
For the poor widows that you leave behind,
Though by the law their goods are all confiscate,
Yet we'll be their good lord, and give 'em them.

CLARIDIANA
O, hell of hells! Why did not we hire some villain to fire our houses?

ROGERO
I thought not of that; my mind was altogether of the gallows.

CLARIDIANA
May the wealth I leave behind me help to damn her!
And as the cursèd fate of courtezan,
What she gleans with her traded art,
May one, as a most due plague, cheat from her
In the last dotage of her tirèd lust,
And leave her an unpitied age of woe!

ROGERO
Amen, amen!

WATCH
I never heard men pray more fervently.

ROGERO
O that a man had the instinct of a lion!
He knows when the lioness plays false to him.
But these solaces, these women, they bring man to grey hairs before he be thirty; yet they cast out such mists of flattery from their breath, that a man's lost again. Sure I fell into my marriage-bed drunk, like the leopard; well, with sober eyes, would I had avoided it!
Come, grave, and hide me from my blasted fame.
O that thou couldst as well conceal my shame!

[Exeunt **AMBO THE DUKE**, with **OFFICERS**.

THAIS
Your pardon and your favour, gracious duke,

[**WOMEN** kneel.

At once we do implore, that have so long
Deceived your royal expectation,
Assurèd that the comic knitting up
Will move your spleen unto the proper use

Of mirth, your natural inclination;
And wipe away the watery-coloured anger
From your enforcèd cheek. Fair lord, beguile
Them and your saf't with a pleasing smile.

DUKE
Now by my life I do: fair ladies, rise;
I ne'er did purpose any other end
To them and these designs. I was inform'd
Of some notorious error as I sat in judgment;
And—do you hear?—these night works require
A cat's eyes to impierce dejected darkness.
Call back the prisoners.

[Re-enter **CLARIDIANA** and **ROGERO**, with **OFFICERS**.

CLARIDIANA
Now what other troubled news, that we must back thus? Has any senator begg'd my pardon upon my
wife's prostitution to him?

ROGERO
What a spite's this; I had kept in my breath of purpose, thinking to go away the quieter, and must we
now back?

DUKE
Since you are to die, we'll give you winding-sheets,
Wherein you shall be shrouded alive,
By which we wind out all these miseries.
Signor Rogero, bestow a while your eye,
And read here of your true wife's chastity.

[Gives him a letter.

ROGERO
Chastity?
I will sooner expect a Jesuit's recantation,
Or the great Turk's conversion, than her chastity.
Pardon, my liege; I will not trust mine eyes:
Women and devils will deceive the wise!

DUKE [To **CLARIDIANA**]
The like, sir, is apparent on your side.

CLARIDIANA
Who? my wife?—chaste? Has your grace your sense? I'll sooner believe a conjuror may say his prayers
with zeal, than her honesty. Had she been an hermaphrodite, I would scarce have given credit to you.
Let him that hath drunk love-drugs trust a woman.
By Heaven, I think the air is not more common!

DUKE
Then we impose a strict command upon you.
On your allegiance read what there is writ.

CLARIDIANA
A writ of error, on my life, my liege!

DUKE
You'll find it so, I fear.

CLARIDIANA
What have we here—the Art of Brachygraphy?

[Looks on the letter.

THAIS
He's stung already:
As if his eyes were turn'd on Perseus' shield,
Their motion's fix'd, like to the pool of Styx.

ABIGAIL
Yonder's our flames; and from the hollow arches
Of his quick eyes comes comet-trains of fire,
Bursting like hidden furies from their caves.

CLARIDIANA [Reading]
Yours till he sleep the sleep of all the world, Rogero.

ROGERO
Marry, and that lethargy seize you! Read again.

[Reads again.

CLARIDIANA
Thy servant so made by his stars, Rogero.
A fire on your wand'ring stars, Rogero!

ROGERO [To **CLARIDIANA**]
Satan, why hast thou tempted my wife?

CLARIDIANA
Peace, seducer; I am branded in the forehead with your star-mark. May the stars drop upon thee, and with their sulphur vapours choke thee, ere thou come at the gallows!

ROGERO
Stretch not my patience, Mahomet.

CLARIDIANA
Termagant, that will stretch thy patience!

ROGERO
Had I known this I would have poison'd thee in the chalice
This morning, when we received the sacrament.

CLARIDIANA
Slave, know'st thou this?

[Showing the ring.

'Tis an appendix to the letter;
But the greater temptation is hidden within.
I will scour thy gorge like a hawk:
Thou shalt swallow thine own stone in this letter,
Seal'd and delivered in the presence of——

[They bustle.

DUKE
Keep them asunder; list to us, we command—

CLARIDIANA
O violent villain! is not thy hand hereto,
And writ in blood to show thy raging lust?

THAIS
Spice of a new halter, when you go a-ranging thus like devils, would you might burn for't as they do!

ROGERO
Thus 'tis to lie with another man's wife: he shall be sure to hear on't again. But we are friends, sweet duck.

[Kisses **THAIS**.

And this shall be my maxim all my life:—
Man never happy is till in a wife.

CLARIDIANA
Here sink our hate lower than any whirlpool;
And this chaste kiss I give thee for thy care,

[Kisses **ABIGAIL**.

Thou fame of women, full as wise as fair.

DUKE

You have saved us a labour in your love.
But, gentlemen, why stood you so prepost'rously?
Would you have headlong run to infamy—
In so defamed a death?

ROGERO
O, my liege, I had rather roar to death with Phalaris' bull, than, Darius-like, to have one of my wings
extend to Atlas, the other to Europe.
What is a cuckold, learn of me:
Few can tell his pedigree,
Nor his subtile nature conster.
Born a man but dies a monster:
Yet great antiquaries say,
They spring from out Methusala,
Who after Noah's flood was found
To have his crest with branches crown'd.
God in Eden's happy shade
This same wondrous creature made.
Then to cut off all mistaking,
Cuckolds are of women's making;
From whose snares, good Lord deliver us!

CLARIDIANA
Amen, amen!
Before I would prove a cuckold, I would endure a winter's pilgrimage in the frozen zone—go stark naked
through Muscovia, where the climate is nine degrees colder than ice. And thus much to all married
men:—
Now I see great reason why
Love should marry jealousy:
Since man's best of life is fame,
He hath need preserve the same;
When 'tis in a woman's keeping,
Let not Argus' eyes be sleeping.
The box unto Pandora given
By the better powers of heaven,
That contains pure chastity,
And each virgin sovereignty,
Wantonly she oped and lost,
Gift whereof a god might boast.
Therefore, shouldst thou Diana wed,
Yet be jealous of her bed.

DUKE
Night, like a masque, is enter'd heaven's great hall,
With thousand torches ushering the way.
To Risus will we consecrate this evening;
Like Mycerinus cheating th' oracle,
We'll make this night the day. Fair joys befall

Us and our actions. Are you pleasèd all?

[Exeunt **OMNES**.

John Marston – A Short Biography

John Marston was born to John and Maria Marston née Guarsi, and baptised on October 7th, 1576 at Wardington, Oxfordshire. His father was an eminent lawyer of the Middle Temple who first practiced in London and then became the counsel to Coventry and later its steward.

Marston entered Brasenose College, Oxford in 1592 and earned his BA in 1594. By 1595, he was in London, living in the Middle Temple. His interests were in poetry and play writing, although his father's will of 1599 hopes that he would not further pursue such vanities.

His brief career in literature began with a foray into the then fashionable genres of erotic epyllion and satire; erotic plays for boy actors to be performed before educated young men and members of the inns of court.

In 1598, he published 'The Metamorphosis of Pigmalion's Image and Certaine Satyres', a book of poetry in imitation of, on the one hand, Ovid, and, on the other, the Satires of Juvenal. He also published 'The Scourge of Villanie', in 1598. (these were issued under the pseudonym "W. Kinsayder.") The satire in these books is even more savage and misanthropic than the prevailing norm for other satirists of the era. Marston's style sometimes bends to the point of unintelligibility: he believed that satire should be rough and obscure. Marston seems to have been enraged by Joseph Hall's claim to be the first satirist in English; Hall comes in for some indirect retribution later in one or more of his satires. Some see William Shakespeare's Thersites and Iago, as well as the mad speeches of King Lear as influenced by 'The Scourge of Villanie'.

Marston had, however, arrived on the literary scene as the fad for verse satire was coming under pressure from the authority's censors. Both the Archbishop of Canterbury and the Bishop of London banned 'The Scourge of Villanie' had it publicly burned, along with copies of works by other satirists, on 4th June 1599.

In September 1599, John Marston began to work for the famed Philip Henslowe as a playwright. Marston proved a good match for the private stage where boy players performed racy dramas for an audience of city gallants and young members of the Inns of Court.

'Histriomastix' has been regarded as his first play; performed by either the Children of Paul's or the students of the Middle Temple in around 1599. Its performance kicked off an episode in literary history commonly known as the 'War of the Theatres'; the literary feud between Marston, Jonson and Dekker that took place between 1599 and 1602.

Around 1600, Marston wrote 'Jack Drum's Entertainment' and 'Antonio and Mellida', and in 1601 he wrote 'Antonio's Revenge', a sequel to the latter play; all three were performed by the company at Paul's. In 1601, he contributed poems to Robert Chester's 'Love's Martyr'. For Henslowe, he may have also collaborated with Dekker, Day, and Haughton on 'Lust's Dominion'.

By 1601, he was well known in London literary circles, particularly in his role as enemy to the equally brilliant and difficult Ben Jonson. Jonson, who reported that Marston had accused him of sexual profligacy, satirized Marston as Clove in 'Every Man Out of His Humour', as Crispinus in 'Poetaster', and as Hedon in 'Cynthia's Revels'. Jonson thought Marston a false poet, a vain, careless writer who plagiarised the works of others and whose works were marked by bizarre diction and ugly neologisms. For his part, Marston used Jonson as the complacent, arrogant critic Brabant Senior in 'Jack Drum's Entertainment' and as the envious, misanthropic playwright and satirist Lampatho Doria in 'What You Will'.

'The Return from Parnassus (II)', an anonymous and satirical play performed at St. John's College, Cambridge in 1601 and 1602, characterised Marston as a poet whose writings see him 'pissing against the world'.

Jonson states that at one point their 'War' boiled over into the physical when he had beaten Marston and taken his pistol. However, the two playwrights were reconciled; Marston wrote a prefatory poem for Jonson's 'Sejanus' in 1605 and dedicated 'The Malcontent' to him.

Beyond this episode Marston's career continued to gather both strength, assets and followers. In 1603, he became a shareholder in the Children of Blackfriars company, at that time known for steadily pushing the boundaries of personal satire, violence, and lewdness on stage. He wrote and produced two plays with the company. The first was 'The Malcontent' in 1603, his most famous play. This work was originally written for the children at Blackfriars and was later taken over by the Kings' Men at the Globe, with additions by John Webster. His second play for the Blackfriars children was 'The Dutch Courtesan', a satire on lust and hypocrisy, in 1604-5.

In 1605, he worked with George Chapman and Ben Jonson on 'Eastward Ho', a satire of popular taste and the vain imaginings of wealth to be found in the colony of Virginia. Chapman and Jonson were arrested for, according to Jonson, a few clauses that offended the Scots, but Marston escaped any imprisonment. Their detainment was brief, and the charges were dropped.

He married Mary Wilkes in 1605, the daughter of the Reverend William Wilkes, one of the chaplains to King James.

In 1606, Marston seems to have had mixed fortunes with the king. At times offending and at others pleasing. In 'Parasitaster, or, The Fawn', he satirized the king specifically. However, in the summer of that year, he put on a production of 'The Dutch Courtesan' for the King of Denmark's visit, with a Latin verse on King James that was presented by hand to the king. Finally, in 1607, he wrote 'The Entertainment at Ashby', a masque for the Earl of Huntingdon.

Marston took the theatre world by surprise when he gave up writing plays in 1609 at the age of thirty-three. He sold his shares in the company of Blackfriars. His departure from the literary scene may have been because of further offence he gave to the king. The king suspended performances at Blackfriars and had Marston imprisoned.

After release he moved into his father-in-law's house to study philosophy. In 1609, he became a reader at the Bodleian library at Oxford. On 24th September he was made a deacon and then a priest on 24th December 1609. In October 1616, Marston was assigned the living of Christchurch, Hampshire.

He died (accounts vary) on either the 24th or 25th June 1634 in London and was buried in the Middle Temple Church.

Tombs at that time were often inscribed with 'Memoriae Sacrum' ('Sacred to the memory') and then the occupants name and a brief account of their achievements. According to Anthony à Wood Marston's tomb stone read 'Oblivioni Sacrum' ('Sacred to Oblivion'), which was probably composed by Marston, and both self-abasing and witty in upturning the tradition.

Marston's reputation through the centuries has varied widely, like that of most of the minor Renaissance dramatists. Both 'The Malcontent' and 'The Dutch Courtesan' remained on stage in altered forms throughout the Restoration.

After the Restoration, Marston's works were largely reduced to literary history. The general resemblance of 'The Malcontent' to 'Hamlet' and Marston's role in the 'War of the Theatres' ensured that his plays would receive some scholarly attention, but they were not performed, nor widely read.

The Romantic movement in English literature unevenly resuscitated Marston's reputation. In his lectures, William Hazlitt praised Marston's genius for satire; however, if the romantic critics were willing to grant Marston's best work a place among the great accomplishments of the age, they remained aware of his inconsistency, what Swinburne would later call his 'uneven and irregular demesne'.

In the twentieth century, however, a few critics were willing to consider Marston as a writer who was very much in control of the world he created. T. S. Eliot saw that this 'irregular demesne' was a part of Marston's world and that "It is ... by giving us the sense of something behind, more real than any of the personages and their action, that Marston establishes himself among the writers of genius".

John Marston – A Concise Bibliography

Plays and production dates

Histriomastix (play), 1599
Antonio and Mellida, London, Paul's theater, 1599–1600.
Jack Drum's Entertainment, London, Paul's theater, 1599/1600.
Antonio's Revenge, London, Paul's theater, 1600.
What You Will, London, Paul's theater, 1601.
The Malcontent, London, Blackfriars Theatre, 1603–1604; Globe Theatre, 1604.
Parasitaster, or The Fawn, London, Blackfriars theater, 1604.
Eastward Ho, by Marston, George Chapman, and Ben Jonson, London, Blackfriars theater, 1604–1605.
The Dutch Courtesan, London, Blackfriars theater, 1605.
The Wonder of Women, or The Tragedy of Sophonisba, London, Blackfriars theater, 1606.
The Spectacle Presented to the Sacred Majesties of Great Britain, and Denmark as They Passed through London, London, 31 July 1606.
The Entertainment of the Dowager-Countess of Darby, Ashby-de-la-Zouch in Leicestershire, 1607.
The Insatiate Countess, by Marston and William Barksted, London, Whitefriars Theatre, c 1608.

Books

The Metamorphosis of Pigmalions Image. And Certaine Satyres.
The Scourge of Villanie. Three Bookes of Satyres (1598; revised and enlarged edition, 1599)
Jacke Drums Entertainment: Or, The Comedie of Pasquill and Katherine (1601)
Loves Martyr: or, Rosalins Complaint, by Marston, Ben Jonson, William Shakespeare, and George Chapman (1601)
The History of Antonio and Mellida (1602)
Antonios Revenge (1602)
The Malcontent (1604)
Eastward Hoe, by Marston, Chapman, and Jonson (1605)
The Dutch Courtezan (1605)
Parasitaster, or The Fawne (1606)
The Wonder of Women, or The Tragedie of Sophonisba (1606)
What You Will (1607)
Histrio-mastix: Or, The Player Whipt (1610)
The Insatiate Countesse, by Marston and William Barksted (1613)
The Workes of Mr. J. Marston (1633); republished as Tragedies and Comedies (1633)
Comedies, Tragi-comedies; & Tragedies, Nonce Collection (1652)
Lust's Dominion, or The Lascivious Queen (probably the same play as The Spanish Moor's Tragedy), by Marston, Thomas Dekker, John Day, and William Haughton (1657)